COLLECTED WORKS OF RENÉ GUÉNON

THE GREAT TRIAD

RENÉ GUÉNON

THE
GREAT TRIAD

Translator
Henry D. Fohr

Editor
Samuel D. Fohr

SOPHIA PERENNIS

HILLSDALE NY

Originally published in French as
La Grande Triade
© Éditions Gallimard 1957
Second edition 2001
Second Impression 2004
First edition 1991, Quinta Essentia, Cambridge
English translation © Sophia Perennis 2001
All rights reserved

Series editor: James R. Wetmore

For information, address:
Sophia Perennis, P.O. Box 611
Hillsdale NY 12529
sophiaperennis.com

Library of Congress Cataloging-in-Publication Data

Guénon, René
[Grande triade. English]
The great triad / René Guénon ; translated by
Henry D. Fohr ; edited by Samuel D. Fohr.

p. cm. — (Collected works of René Guénon)
Includes index.
ISBN 0 900588 07 1 (pbk: alk. paper)
ISBN 0 900588 40 3 (cloth: alk. paper)
1. Three (The number). 2. Taoism. I. Fohr, Henry D.
II. Fohr, S.D., 1943– III. Title.
IV. Guénon, René. Works. English. 2001
BF1623.P9 P813 2001
299'.5142—dc21   2001005885

THE PUBLISHER
GIVES SPECIAL THANKS TO
HENRY D. AND JENNIE L. FOHR
FOR MAKING THIS EDITION POSSIBLE

CONTENTS

EDITORIAL NOTE

THE PAST CENTURY HAS WITNESSED an erosion of earlier cultural values as well as a blurring of the distinctive characteristics of the world's traditional civilizations, giving rise to philosophic and moral relativism, multiculturalism, and dangerous fundamentalist reactions. As early as the 1920s, the French metaphysician René Guénon (1886–1951) had diagnosed these tendencies and presented what he believed to be the only possible reconciliation of the legitimate, although apparently conflicting, demands of outward religious forms, 'exoterisms', with their essential core, 'esoterism'. His works are characterized by a foundational critique of the modern world coupled with a call for intellectual reform; a renewed examination of metaphysics, the traditional sciences, and symbolism, with special reference to the ultimate unanimity of all spiritual traditions; and finally, a call to the work of spiritual realization. Despite their wide influence, translation of Guénon's works into English has so far been piecemeal. The *Sophia Perennis* edition is intended to fill the urgent need to present them in a more authoritative and systematic form. A complete list of Guénon's works, given in the order of their original publication in French, follows this note.

Guénon's *The Great Triad* was the last book to appear during his lifetime. Even for his regular readers, this book contained largely new material, as did his *The Metaphysical Principles of the Infinitesimal Calculus*, published the same year. The author here refers especially to the Chinese tradition, principally in its Taoist form (though touching on Confucianism as well), in which the 'Great Triad' is defined as Heaven-Man-Earth. It is as much a cosmological as a metaphysical doctrine that is implied in this ternary of the 'three worlds'. In spite of its Taoist title, however, the work draws heavily on Hermetic teachings, Hindu and Buddhist metaphysics, and Masonic symbolism, not to mention doctrines from Judaism,

Christianity. and Islam. It is also Guenon's most comprehensive exposition of the science of Alchemy.

Guénon often uses words or expressions set off in 'scare quotes'. To avoid clutter, single quotation marks have been used throughout. As for transliterations, Guénon was more concerned with phonetic fidelity than academic usage. The system adopted here reflects the views of scholars familiar both with the languages and Guénon's writings. Brackets indicate editorial insertions, or, within citations, Guénon's additions. Wherever possible, references have been updated, and English editions substituted.

The Great Triad first appeared in English in 1991, translated by Peter Kingsley for QuintaEssentia . The present translation is based on the work of Henry Fohr, edited by his son Samuel Fohr. The text was checked for accuracy and further revised by Patrick Moore. For help with selected chapters and proofreading thanks go to John Champoux, John Herlihy, and Allan Dewar. A special debt of thanks is owed to Cecil Bethell, who revised and proofread the text at several stages and provided the index. Cover design by Michael Buchino and Gray Henry, based on a drawing of a Sun-bird and Sun-door motif from eighth-century (BC) Cyprus, by Guénon's friend and collaborator Ananda K. Coomaraswamy.

THE WORKS
OF RENÉ GUÉNON

PREFACE

FROM THE VERY TITLE of this study it will doubtless be clear to many that it is concerned chiefly with the symbolism of the Far-Eastern tradition because of the widely known role played in this tradition by the ternary composed of the terms 'Heaven-Earth-Man' (*T'ien-Ti-Jen*), which is commonly designated by the name 'Triad', even if the meaning and influence of this term—which is precisely what we propose to explain here, while indicating moreover the correspondences to be found in other traditional forms—is not always understood exactly. We have already devoted a chapter of another book to this subject,[1] but it deserves to be treated at greater length. It is also well known that there exists in China a 'secret society', or at least what is generally called such, to which the West has given the name 'Triad'; but as it is not our intention to concern ourselves especially with this organization, it will be well to say a few words about it at the outset, so as to avoid having to return to it in the course of our exposition.[2]

The true name of the organization in question is *T'ien Ti Huei*, which can be translated as 'Society of Heaven and Earth' provided that, for reasons we explained elsewhere,[3] due reservations are made regarding the use of the word 'society', for although it is a relatively outward order, it is far from having all the special characteristics

---

1. *The Symbolism of the Cross*, chap. 28.

2. Details of the organization in question, and of its ritual and symbols (especially the numerical symbols it uses), are to be found in a work by Lieutenant-Colonel B. Favre entitled *Les Sociétés secrètes en Chine*. This work was written from a profane point of view, but the author at least perceived certain things that are usually overlooked by sinologists; and even though he is far from having resolved all the questions he raises, he nevertheless has the merit of having raised them very clearly. See also Matgioi, *La Voie rationnelle*, chap. 7.

3. *Perspectives on Initiation*, chap. 12.

inevitably evoked by this word in the modern Western world. It will be noticed that only the first two terms of the traditional Triad figure in this title; this is because the organization itself (*huei*), by virtue of its members understood in a collective as well as an individual sense, here takes the place of the third term, as will become better understood from the following considerations.[4] It is often said that this same organization is known by many other names as well, among which are some where the idea of the ternary is explicitly mentioned;[5] but in fact this is inaccurate: these names properly apply only to particular branches or to temporary 'emanations' of this organization, which appear at a certain moment in history and disappear as soon as they have completed the role for which they were especially intended.[6]

We have already indicated elsewhere the true nature of all organizations of this kind;[7] they must always be considered as proceeding, in the final analysis, from the Taoist hierarchy, which creates them and which directs them invisibly for the sake of some more or less outward activity in which it could not itself directly intervene by virtue of the principle of 'non-action' (*wu wei*), according to which the role of the hierarchy is essentially that of the 'unmoved mover', that is, the center that governs the movement of all things without participating in this movement. Most sinologists are quite naturally

---

4. It should be noted that *jen* means both 'man' and 'humanity'; moreover, from the point of view of applications to the social order, it signifies the 'solidarity' of the race, whose practical realization is one of the contingent aims the organization in question sets itself.

5. Especially the 'Three Rivers' (*San Ho*) and the 'Three Points' (*San Tien*); use of this last expression is obviously one of the factors that have led certain people to search for connections between the 'Triad' and Western initiatic organizations such as Masonry and the Compagnonnage.

6. This essential distinction must never be lost to view by those who wish to consult the book that we cited by Lieutenant-Colonel B. Favre, where it is unfortunately neglected, to the point that the author seems to consider all these names as pure and simple equivalents. In fact, most of the details he provides on the subject of the 'Triad' really only concern one of its emanations, the *Hong Huei*; and in particular it is the *Hong Huei* alone, and most definitely not the *T'ien Ti Huei*, which can only have been founded toward the end of the seventeenth or the beginning of the eighteenth century, that is, at a very recent date.

7. See *Perspectives on Initiation*, chaps. 12 and 46.

ignorant of this, for their studies, given the special point of view from which they are undertaken, could hardly teach them that in the Far East everything of an esoteric or initiatic order, to whatever degree, necessarily relates to Taoism; but what is nonetheless rather curious is that even those who have discovered in these 'secret societies' a Taoist influence, have not been able to go any further and have not drawn any important conclusions from this. Noting at the same time the presence of other elements, particularly Buddhist, they hasten to pronounce the word 'syncretism', little suspecting that this word designates something altogether opposed, on the one hand to the eminently 'synthetic' mentality of the Chinese people, and on the other to the initiatic spirit from which the organizations in question obviously derive, even if in this respect these are only forms somewhat far removed from the center.[8] Certainly, we do not mean that all the members of these relatively outward organizations must be aware of the fundamental unity of all traditions; but those who are behind these organizations and inspire them necessarily possess it in their capacity as 'true men' (*chen jen*), and it is this that allows them to introduce, when circumstances are opportune or advantageous, formal elements properly belonging to other traditions.[9]

We must dwell a little in this regard on the use of elements of Buddhist provenance, not so much because they are unquestionably the most numerous, something easily explained by the wide diffusion of Buddhism in China as well as in the entire Far East, but because there is a deeper reason for this use which makes it particularly interesting and without which, indeed, this very diffusion of Buddhism might not have taken place. One could without difficulty find numerous examples of this use, but apart from those which themselves possess only a more or less secondary importance, and whose value lies above all precisely in their sheer number, which

---

8. Cf. *Perspectives on Initiation*, chap. 6.

9. This sometimes even includes traditions most foreign to the Far East, such as Christianity, as can be seen from the case of the association called 'Great Peace' or *T'ai P'ing*, which is one of the more recent emanations of the *Pai Lien Huei*, something we shall consider shortly.

serves to attract and hold the attention of the outside observer and thereby to divert it from what is of a more essential character,[10] there is at least one extremely clear example which bears on something more than mere details: this is the use of the symbol of the 'white lotus' in the very title of the other Far-Eastern organization that is situated at the same level as the *T'ien Ti Huei*.[11] In fact, *Pai Lien Chai* or *Pai Lien Tsung*, the name of a Buddhist school, and *Pai Lien Chiao* or *Pai Lien Huei*, the name of the organization in question, designate two altogether different things; yet there is a kind of deliberate ambiguity in the adoption of this particular title by this organization of Taoist origin, just as there also is in certain rites of Buddhist appearance, or again in the 'legends' in which Buddhist monks almost constantly play a more or less important role. It can be seen quite clearly from an example like this how Buddhism can serve as a 'cover' for Taoism, and how it is thereby able to spare Taoism the disadvantage of manifesting itself outwardly more than would have been fitting for a doctrine which by definition must always be reserved for a restricted elite. This is why Taoism could promote the spread of Buddhism in China, without the need to invoke affinities of origin which exist only in the imagination of certain orientalists; and it could do this all the better because the esoteric and the exoteric parts of the Far-Eastern tradition had been established as two branches of doctrine as profoundly different as Taoism and Confucianism, and it was easy to find room between the two for something intermediate. It should be added that Chinese Buddhism was itself in large measure influenced by Taoism, as can be seen from the adoption by some of its schools, notably the *Ch'an* school,[12] of certain manifestly Taoist methods, and also from the assimilation of certain symbols of no less essentially Taoist

10. The notion of a so-called 'syncretism' in Chinese 'secret societies' is a particular case of the results obtained by this means when the outward observer happens to be a modern Westerner.

11. We say 'the other' because there are really only two; all the associations known outwardly are really only branches or emanations of one or the other.

12. A Chinese transcription of the Sanskrit word *Dhyāna*, meaning 'contemplation'; this school is more commonly known under the name *Zen*, which is the Japanese form of the same word.

provenance, such as *Kuan Yin* for example; and it is hardly necessary to remark that it is thus yet more qualified to play the role which we have just noted.

There are also other elements whose presence even the most ardent partisans of the theory of 'borrowings' could hardly explain as 'syncretism', and which have remained an insoluble enigma for lack of any initiatic knowledge among those wishing to study Chinese 'secret societies'; we are referring to those which bring about sometimes striking similarities between these organizations and those of the same order belonging to other traditional forms. Some have gone so far as to entertain, in particular, the hypothesis of a common origin for both the 'Triad' and Freemasonry, without being able to support it with any solid reasons, which certainly is not at all surprising. The idea need not be rejected absolutely, but this is on the condition that it be understood in a sense altogether different from what they have in mind, that is, that it be referred, not to some more or less distant origin, but solely to the identity of the principles governing every initiation, whether of the East or of the West; to discover the true explanation for this similarity it is necessary to go back well before the beginning of history, that is, to the primordial tradition itself.[13] As to certain similarities that seem to bear on more particular points, we will only say that things like the use of numerical symbolism, for example, or again the use of 'architectural' symbolism, are in no way peculiar to this or that initiatic form, but are on the contrary among those found everywhere, with mere differences of adaptation, because they relate to sciences or arts that exist also, and with the same 'sacred' character, in all traditions. They really belong, therefore, to the domain of initiation in general, and consequently, where the Far East is concerned, they properly belong to the domain of Taoism; if the

---

13. It is true that initiation as such only became necessary at a certain period in the cycle of terrestrial humanity and as a consequence of the spiritual degeneration of the generality of humankind; but all that it includes originally constituted the higher part of the primordial tradition, just as, analogically and with reference to a cycle much more limited in time and space, everything implicit in Taoism constituted from the very beginning the higher part of the one and only tradition which existed in the Far East prior to the separation of the two parts, esoteric and exoteric.

adventitious elements, Buddhist or otherwise, are rather a 'mask', these on the contrary belong to what is truly essential.

When we speak here of Taoism, and when we say that such and such a thing belongs to it, which is the case for most of the considerations we will be examining in the present study, we must specify further that this must be understood in reference to the Far-Eastern tradition in its present state, for minds too prone to view everything 'historically' might be tempted to conclude that it is a question of ideas not to be found prior to the formation of what is properly called Taoism, whereas very far from that, they are to be found continually in all that is known of the Chinese tradition since the most remote period to which one can go back, that is, from the time of Fu Hsi. This is because in reality Taoism has made no 'innovations' in the esoteric and initiatic domain, any more than Confucianism has in the exoteric and social domain; each in its own order is only a 're-adaptation' necessitated by conditions thanks to which the tradition in its original form was no longer integrally understood.[14] From that time, one part of the earlier tradition entered into Taoism and another into Confucianism, and this state of affairs has continued down to the present day; to relate certain conceptions to Taoism and others to Confucianism is in no way to attribute them to something more or less comparable to what Westerners would call 'systems', and is fundamentally nothing more than to say that they belong respectively to the esoteric and the exoteric parts of the Far-Eastern tradition.

We shall not speak again explicitly of the *T'ien Ti Huei* except when there is need to clarify certain particular points, for this is not what we propose; but what we shall say in the course of this study, beyond its much more general purview, will show implicitly on what principles this organization rests, in virtue of its very name, and will thereby allow one to understand how, despite its outwardness, it has a truly initiatic character that assures its members at least a virtual participation in the Taoist tradition. In fact, the role

14. It is known that the constitution of these two different branches of the Far-Eastern tradition dates from the sixth century BC, the time in which Lao Tzu and Confucius lived.

assigned to man as the third term of the Triad is, at a certain level, properly that of 'true man' (*chen jen*) and, at another, that of 'transcendent man' (*chün jen*), thus indicating the respective goals of the 'lesser mysteries' and the 'greater mysteries', that is, the very goals of all initiation. Doubtless, that organization in itself is not among those that allow these goals to be effectively attained; but it can at least prepare those who are 'qualified' for them, however far off they may be, and it thus constitutes one of the 'forecourts' that can give them access to the Taoist hierarchy, whose degrees are none other than those of initiatic realization itself.

1

TERNARY AND TRINITY

BEFORE TAKING UP the study of the Far-Eastern Triad, it is advisable to be carefully on guard against the misconceptions and false comparisons prevalent in the West which arise above all from the desire to see in every traditional ternary, whatever it may be, a more or less exact equivalent of the Christian Trinity. This error belongs not only to theologians, who could be excused for wishing to bring everything back to their own special point of view; what is more peculiar is that it is even committed by people who are strangers or even hostile to every religion, including Christianity, but who, because of the milieu in which they live, are more familiar with it than with other traditional forms (which is not to say that they really understand it much better), and who as a result more or less unconsciously make of it a kind of term of comparison to which they try to refer everything else. Among the examples one could give of these unwarranted assimilations, that most frequently encountered concerns the Hindu *Trimurti*, which is nowadays even given the name of 'Trinity'; yet if misunderstandings are to be avoided, it is indispensable that this latter term be reserved exclusively for the Christian concept which it has always been properly intended to designate. In reality, both cases concern three divine aspects, but any resemblance ends there; since these aspects are in no way the same in either case, and since their distinctions do not refer in any way to the same point of view, it is wholly impossible to make the three terms of one of the ternaries correspond with those of the other.[1]

---

1. Of the different ternaries envisaged in Hindu tradition, that which could in certain respects be most validly compared with the Christian Trinity, although the

The first condition for assimilating two ternaries belonging to different traditional forms is the possibility of establishing a valid term by term correspondence; in other words, their respective terms would have to have equivalence or similar relationships between them. Moreover, this condition is not in itself sufficient to allow a pure and simple identification of the two ternaries, for it is quite possible for there to be a correspondence between two ternaries which, even though being thus of the same type, so to speak, are situated on different levels, either in the principial order or in the order of manifestation, or even respectively in one and the other. Of course, this can equally be so for ternaries envisaged by one and the same tradition, but in this case it is easier to guard against a false identification, for it goes without saying that the ternaries in question are not simply duplicates, while, where different traditions are concerned, there is the temptation, as soon as appearances seem to lend themselves to it, to establish equivalences which may not at root be justified. However that may be, the error is never so serious as when it consists in identifying ternaries that have nothing in common except the fact of being ternaries, that is, sets of three terms, and where the relationships among the three terms are completely different. In order to know what one has, therefore, it is necessary first to determine what kind of ternary exists in each case, even before asking what order of reality it relates to; if two ternaries are of the same type, then there will be a correspondence between them, and if in addition they both belong to the same order—or, to be more precise, the same level—there may be a case of identity if they are formulated from the same point of view, or at the very least a case of equivalence, if the point of view is somewhat different. It is above all this failure to draw the essential distinctions between different types of ternary that has led to all sorts of fanciful comparisons without the slightest bearing on reality, such as those that so delight the occultists, for whom it is enough to come upon some group of three terms to promptly try to

---

point of view will naturally still be very different, is the ternary *Sat-Chit-Ānanda*. See *Man and His Becoming according to the Vedānta*, chap. 14.

make it correspond to all the other groups containing the same number of terms which they may have found elsewhere; their works are replete with tables drawn up in this way, some of which are veritable prodigies of incoherence and confusion.[2]

As we shall see more fully in due course, the Far-Eastern Triad belongs to the type of ternary formed by two complementary terms plus a third term which is the product of their union, or, if it be preferred, from their reciprocal action and reaction; if one takes as symbols images borrowed from the human domain, the three terms of such a ternary can in a general way be described as Father, Mother, and Son.[3] Now, it is manifestly impossible to make these three terms correspond to the three terms of the Christian Trinity, where the first two are not at all complementary or in any way symmetrical, but where on the contrary the second derives from the first alone; as for the third, although it indeed proceeds from the other two, that procession is not in any way conceived as a generation or a filiation, but constitutes another, essentially different relationship, however one might wish to define it—a matter we need not explore more precisely here. What can lead to some ambiguity is that here also two of the terms are designated as Father and Son; but first of all, the Son is the second term and not the third, and next the third term cannot in any way correspond to the Mother, be this only—even were other reasons lacking—because it comes after the Son and not before him. It is true that certain more or less heterodox Christian sects have claimed that the Holy Spirit is feminine, and because of this have tried precisely to attribute to it a character

2. What we are saying here about groups of three terms applies just as well to those that contain another number and which are often associated with each other in the same arbitrary fashion merely because the number of terms they consist of happens to be the same, without the real nature of the terms being taken into consideration. There are even some who for the sake of discovering imaginary correspondences go so far as to artificially fabricate groupings that traditionally have no meaning whatsoever; a typical example is the case of Malfatti of Montereggio who in his *Mathesis* gathered together the names of ten completely heterogeneous principles taken from here and there in the Hindu tradition and thought he had found an equivalent to the ten *Sephiroth* of the Hebrew Kabbalah.

3. The ancient Egyptian triads, of which the best known is that of Osiris, Isis, and Horus, also fall within this class of ternary.

comparable with that of the Mother; but it is very likely that they were influenced by a false assimilation of the Trinity to a ternary of the type we just discussed, which would show that errors of this kind do not belong exclusively to the moderns. Furthermore, and still keeping to this subject, the feminine character thus attributed to the Holy Spirit in no way agrees with the essentially masculine and 'paternal' role which, quite the contrary, it incontestably plays in the generation of Christ; and this observation is important for us because it is precisely here and not in the idea of the Trinity that we can find in Christianity something that corresponds in a certain way, and with all the reservations different points of view always require, to ternaries of the same type as the Far-Eastern Triad.[4]

In fact, the 'working of the Holy Spirit' in the generation of Christ corresponds properly to the 'actionless' activity of *Purusha*, or of 'Heaven', in the language of the Far-Eastern tradition; the Virgin, on the other hand, is a perfect image of *Prakriti*, which the same tradition designates as 'Earth';[5] and as for Christ himself, his identity with 'Universal Man' is even more obvious.[6] Should one wish therefore to find a concordance here, it will be necessary to say, using the terms of Christian theology, that the Triad does not relate to the generation of the Word *ad intra*, which is contained in the idea of the Trinity, but rather to its generation *ad extra*, that is to say, following the Hindu tradition, to the birth of the *Avatāra* in the manifested world.[7] This is moreover easy to understand, for, starting

---

4. Let us note incidentally that the apparent general belief that the Christian tradition does not envisage any other ternary than the Trinity is wrong; on the contrary, many others can be found, and we have here one of the most important examples.

5. This is particularly evident in symbolic representations of the 'Black Virgin', the color black here symbolizing the non-differentiation of *materia prima*.

6. In this connection we will repeat once again that we have not the least intention of disputing the 'historicity' of certain facts as such, but that, quite to the contrary, we consider historical facts themselves to be symbols of a reality of a higher order, and it is only in this respect that they hold any interest for us.

7. The mother of the *Avatāra* is *Māyā*, who is the same as *Prakriti*; we shall not dwell on the connection that certain people wish to establish between the names *Maya* and *Maria*, and we mention it as a mere curiosity [see *Traditional Forms and Cosmic Cycles*, pt. 4, chap. 2, n12].

from the idea of *Purusha* and *Prakriti* or their equivalents, the Triad can only be situated on the side of manifestation, of which its first two terms are the two poles;[8] and it can be said that it fills manifestation entirely, for as we shall see later Man appears there veritably as the synthesis of the 'ten thousand beings', that is, of all that is contained in the totality of universal Existence.

8. See *Man and His Becoming according to the Vedānta*, chap. 4.

2

DIFFERENT TYPES
OF TERNARY

WHAT we have just said already determines the meaning of the Triad at the same time that it shows the need to establish a clear distinction between ternaries of different types. Indeed, there can be many types, for it is evident that three terms can be grouped together according to very different relationships; but we will dwell on only the two principal types, not just because they present the most general character, but also because they relate most directly to the subject of our study. Moreover, the remarks we shall make in this connection will enable us to dismiss once and for all the flagrant error of those who claim to see a 'dualism' in the Far-Eastern tradition. One of these types is where the ternary is formed by a first principle (at least in a relative sense) from which derive two opposite, or rather complementary, terms, for even where there appears to be an opposition that is valid at a certain level or in a certain domain, complementarity corresponds to a deeper point of view and is consequently more truly in conformity to the real nature of the ternary in question. Such a ternary can be represented in the form of a triangle whose apex is above (figure 1).

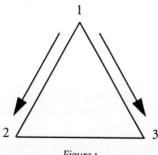

Figure 1

The other type of ternary is where the ternary is formed, as we said earlier, of two complementary terms and their product or resultant, and it is to this type that the Far-Eastern Triad belongs;

contrary to the foregoing, this ternary can be represented by a triangle whose base is placed at the top (figure 2).[1] If we compare these
two triangles, it becomes apparent that the second is as it were a
reflection of the first, which indi-
cates that between corresponding ternaries there is an analogy
in the true sense of the word, that
is, one having to be applied
inversely; and indeed, if we begin
by considering the two complementary terms, between which
there is necessarily a symmetry,
we see that in the first case the
ternary is completed by their

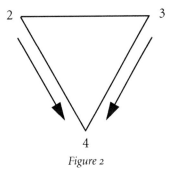

Figure 2

principle and in the second, on the contrary, by their resultant, so
that the two complementaries are respectively after and before the
term which, being of another order, is as it were isolated with
respect to them;[2] and it is evident that in every case it is this third
term that gives the ternary as such all its significance.

Now, what must be understood before going further is that there
can be no question of 'dualism' in any doctrine unless two opposite
or complementary terms (and they would be conceived rather as
opposites) are posited at the outset and regarded as ultimate and
irreducible, without any derivation from a common principle,
something that obviously excludes consideration of any ternary of
the first type; thus only ternaries of the second type could be found
in such a doctrine since these, as we have already pointed out, relate
only to the domain of manifestation, it can immediately be seen that
any 'dualism' is necessarily at the same time a 'naturalism'. But the
fact of acknowledging the existence of a duality and situating it in

---

1. It will shortly be seen why in the second diagram we number the three terms
2–3–4 rather than 1–2–3, as in the first.

2. Moreover, this is made clear in the two diagrams by the direction of the
arrows, in the first diagram going from the apex at the top to the base, and in the
second from the base to the apex at the bottom. It could also be said that the number (3) of the terms breaks down into 1 + 2 in the first case and to 2 + 1 in the second, and it is clear here that, if these two figures are equivalent from a quantitative
point of view, they are most certainly not from a qualitative point of view.

the place that really belongs to it, in no way constitutes a 'dualism' as long as the two terms of this duality proceed from a single principle belonging as such to a higher order of reality; and this is especially the case with the first of all dualities, that of universal Essence and Substance. These arise from a polarization of Being or of principial Unity and through their interaction all manifestation is produced. It is the two terms of this first duality that are designated *Purusha* and *Prakriti* in the Hindu tradition and Heaven (*T'ien*) and Earth (*Ti*) in the Far-Eastern tradition; but neither, any more than any other orthodox tradition, loses sight of the higher principle from which they derive. We have amply explained this on other occasions with regard to the Hindu tradition; as for the Far-Eastern tradition, it envisages no less explicitly a common principle of Heaven and Earth,[3] what it calls the 'Great Extreme' (*T'ai Chi*), in which they are indissolubly united in an 'undivided' and 'non-distinct'[4] state prior to all differentiation,[5] and which is pure Being, identified as such with the 'Great Unity' (*T'ai I*).[6] Moreover, *T'ai Chi*, Being or transcendent Unity, itself presupposes another principle—*Wu Chi*, Non-Being or the metaphysical Zero;[7] but this cannot enter into relationship with anything so as to become the first term of any ternary, for any relationship of this sort is possible only if it starts with the affirmation of Being or Unity.[8] Thus we finally have, first of all a ternary

3. And also of course the terms of all the other more particular dualities which in the final analysis are always only specifications of these, so that directly or indirectly they all derive ultimately from the same principle.

4. This principial non-distinction must not be confused with the potential non-distinction which belongs only to Substance or *materia prima*.

5. It must be understood that this is not a temporal anteriority or a succession in any mode of duration.

6. The character *Chi* literally designates the 'summit' of a building; thus *T'ai I* is said to reside symbolically in the pole star, which is in fact the 'summit' of the visible heavens and as such naturally represents that of the entire Cosmos.

7. *Wu Chi* corresponds to the neuter and supreme *Brahma* of the Hindu tradition (*Parabrahma*), and *T'ai Chi* to *Īshvara* or the 'non-supreme' *Brahma* (*Aparabrahma*).

8. Above every other principle there remains the *Tao*, which in its most universal sense is both Non-Being and Being, but this is not really different from Non-Being insofar as this contains Being, which is itself the first principle of all manifestation, and is polarized into Essence and Substance (or Heaven and Earth) in order to effectively produce this manifestation.

of the first type formed of *T'ai Chi*, *T'ien*, and *Ti*, and next a ternary of the second type formed of *T'ien*, *Ti*, and *Jen*, which is the one customarily designated as the 'Great Triad'; under these circumstances, it is perfectly incomprehensible that some can have attributed a 'dualistic' character to the Far-Eastern tradition.

Consideration of the two ternaries we have just spoken of, which share the two complementary principles, leads us to certain other important remarks. The two inverted triangles that respectively represent them can be regarded as having the same base, and if they are drawn as united by this common base, it will be seen first that the two ternaries together form a quaternary, since two terms are the same in both so that there are only four distinct terms, and next that the last term of this quaternary, located on the vertical descending from the first term and symmetrical with it with respect to the base, appears as a reflection of this first term, the plane of this reflection being represented by the base itself, which is the median plane on

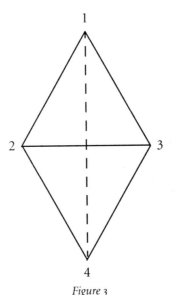

Figure 3

which are located the two complementary terms that issue from the first term and produce the last (figure 3).[9] This is basically quite easy to understand, for on the one hand the two complementaries are contained principially in the first term, so that their respective natures, even when seemingly contrary, are really only the result of a differentiation of the nature of that term; and, on the other hand, the last term, being the product of the two complementaries, participates in both at once, which amounts to saying that in a way it

9. The figure thus formed has certain quite remarkable geometrical properties that we will mention in passing. The two equilateral triangles opposed by their common base are inscribed in two equal circumferences, each of which passes through the center of the other; the chord joining their points of intersection is naturally the common base of the two triangles, and the two arcs subtended by this

combines in itself their two natures, so that it is at its own particular level like an image of the first term; and these considerations lead us to clarify even further the relationship that the different terms have among themselves.

We just saw that the two extreme terms of the quaternary, which are at the same time respectively the first term of the first ternary and the last term of the second, are both by their nature intermediaries as it were between the two others, although for opposite reasons: in both cases they unite and reconcile within themselves the elements of the complementarism, but one does this as principle, the other as resultant. To make this intermediary character clearer we can depict the terms of each ternary in a linear arrangement:[10] in the first case, the first term is located at the middle of the line that joins the two others, to which it gives birth simultaneously through

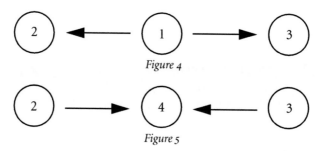

Figure 4

Figure 5

a centrifugal movement in both directions which constitutes what can be called its polarization (figure 4); in the second case, the two

---

chord and marking off the area common to the two circles form the figure called *mandorla* ('almond') or *vesica piscis,* which is well known in the architectural and sigillary symbolism of the Middle Ages. In ancient Masonry, the total number of degrees of these two circumferences, or 360 x 2 = 720, furnished the answer to the question concerning the length of the 'cable-tow'; this special term cannot be translated, first, because it has no exact equivalent in French, and then because phonetically it has a double meaning which evokes (by assimilation with the Arabic *qabaltu*) the initiatic pledge, so that it expresses, one might say, a 'bond' in every sense of the word.

10. This figure can be considered to result from the projection of each of the preceding triangles onto a plane perpendicular to its own and passing through its base.

complementary terms produce by a centripetal movement that proceeds from both at once a resultant which is the last term and which
is also located at the middle of the line that joins them (figure 5); the
principle and resultant thus both occupy a central position with
respect to the two complementaries, and this fact
is particularly worth remembering in view of the
considerations to follow.

This must also be added: two contrary or complementary terms (which fundamentally are
always more complementary than contrary in
their essential reality) can be, according to the
case, either horizontally opposed (opposition of
right and left) or vertically opposed (opposition
of higher and lower), as we have noted elsewhere.[11] Horizontal opposition is that between
two terms which, occupying the same degree of
reality, are so to speak symmetrical in every
respect; vertical opposition indicates on the contrary a hierarchization between the two terms,
which while symmetrical as complementaries, are
nonetheless such that one must be considered as
higher and the other lower. It is important to note
that, in this last case, one cannot place between
the two complementaries or in the middle of the

Figure 6

line that joins them the first term of a ternary of the first type, but
only the third term of a ternary of the second type, for the principle
can never be situated at a level lower than that of the two terms that
derive from it but is necessarily higher than both, while the resultant, on the contrary, is truly intermediary in this respect also; and
this last is the case of the Far-Eastern Triad, which can thus be laid
out in the form of a vertical line (figure 6).[12] In fact, Essence and

11. *The Reign of Quantity and the Signs of the Times*, chap. 30.
12. In this figure we represent the higher term (Heaven) by a circle and the
lower term (Earth) by a square, which is, as we shall see, in agreement with the Far-
Eastern tradition; as for the middle term (Man), he is represented by a cross, this
being, as we have explained elsewhere, the symbol of 'Universal Man' (cf. *The Symbolism of the Cross*).

universal Substance are, respectively, the upper pole and the lower pole of manifestation, and it could be said that one is properly speaking above and the other below all existence; furthermore, when they are designated as Heaven and Earth, this is even expressed in the most exact fashion in the sensible appearances that serve as their symbols.[13]

Thus all manifestation is situated entirely between these two poles; and naturally the same applies to Man, who is not only part of that manifestation but who is symbolically its very center, and who for this reason synthesizes it in its totality. Thus Man, placed between Heaven and Earth, must be envisaged first of all as the product or resultant of their reciprocal influences; but then, by virtue of the dual nature he has from both, he becomes the middle term or 'mediator' which unites them and which is, so to speak, using a symbolism we shall return to later, the 'bridge' leading from the one to the other. These two different points of view can be expressed by a simple modification of the order in which the terms of the Triad are enumerated: if we express them in the sequence 'Heaven, Earth, Man', Man appears as the Son of Heaven and Earth; but if we express them in the sequence 'Heaven, Man, Earth', he appears as the Mediator between Heaven and Earth.

13. That is why the 'summit of Heaven' (*T'ien Chi*) is also, as we pointed out in an earlier note, the summit of the Cosmos in its entirety.

3

HEAVEN
AND EARTH

'HEAVEN covers, Earth supports'; so runs the traditional formula
which defines with great conciseness the roles of these two complementary principles, and which symbolically defines their positions,
respectively higher and lower, in relation to the 'ten thousand
beings', that is, to the totality of universal manifestation.[1] Thus are
indicated, on one hand, the 'non-acting' character of the activity of
Heaven or *Purusha*,[2] and on the other hand the passivity of Earth or
Prakriti, which is properly a 'ground'[3] or 'support' of manifestation,[4] and consequently also a plane of resistance and arrest for the
celestial forces or influences acting in a descending direction. Moreover, this can be applied at every level of existence, since for every
state of manifestation one can envisage an essence and substance in
a relative sense, which are the principles corresponding to what

1. We have indicated elsewhere why the number 'ten thousand' is taken to symbolically represent the indefinite (*Metaphysical Principles of the Infinitesimal Calculus*, chap. 9). On the subject of the Heaven that 'covers', let us recall that an identical
symbolism contained in the Greek word *Ouranos* is the equivalent of the Sanskrit
Varuna (from the root *var*, 'to cover'), and also in the Latin *Caelum*, derived from
caelare ('to conceal' or 'cover'). See *The King of the World*, chap. 7.

2. The 'working of the Holy Spirit', about which we spoke earlier, is sometimes
designated in theological language by the term *obumbratio* [over-shadowing],
which expresses fundamentally the same idea.

3. The English word *ground* renders even more exactly and completely than the
corresponding French word [*terrain*] what we mean here.

4. Cf. the etymological meaning of the word 'substance', literally 'that which
stands beneath'.

universal Essence and Substance are for the totality of states of manifestation.[5]

In the Universal, and viewed from their common principle, Heaven and Earth relate respectively to 'active perfection' (*Ch'ien*) and 'passive perfection' (*K'un*), though neither is Perfection in the absolute sense since there is already a distinction that perforce implies a limitation. Viewed from manifestation they are solely Essence and Substance, and as such situated at a lesser degree of universality because they are such precisely only in relation to manifestation.[6] In every case, at whatever level their correlation is considered, Heaven and Earth are always respectively an active principle and passive principle, or, according to the symbolism most generally used here, a masculine principle and a feminine principle, which is indeed the very type of complementarism par excellence. It is from this that in general all their other characteristics derive, which are as it were secondary to this; however, we must be on our guard here against certain confusions of attributes that could lead to errors, and which moreover are fairly frequent in traditional symbolism wherever it is a question of the relationships between complementary principles. We shall have to return to this point later, particularly in connection with the numerical symbols linked to Heaven and Earth.

It is well-known that in a complementarism whose two terms are envisaged as active and passive with respect to one another, the active term will generally be symbolized by a vertical line and the passive term by a horizontal line;[7] Heaven and Earth are also sometimes represented according to this symbolism. But in this case the two lines do not intersect as they would ordinarily to form a cross,

5. This will help us in particular to understand later [see chapter 14] how the role of 'mediator' can in fact be attributed both to 'true man' as well as to 'transcendent man', while without this observation it might seem as if it should be applied to the latter exclusively.

6. Cf. *The Symbolism of the Cross*, chap. 23. The first of the two points of view indicated here is strictly speaking metaphysical, whereas the second is more cosmological, or, to be more precise, is the very starting-point for every traditional cosmology.

7. See *The Symbolism of the Cross*, chap. 6.

because it is obvious that the symbol of Heaven must be placed entirely above that of the Earth: it is therefore a perpendicular having its foot on the horizontal,[8] and these two lines can be considered as the altitude and base of a triangle whose lateral sides starting from the 'summit of Heaven' effectively determine the measure of the Earth's surface, that is, delimit the 'ground' that serves as the support of manifestation (figure 7).[9]

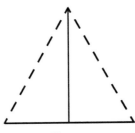

Figure 7

However, the geometric representation most frequently encountered in the Far-Eastern tradition is that which associates circular forms with Heaven and square forms with Earth, as we have already explained elsewhere.[10] Let us only recall that the descending movement of a cycle of manifestation (and this at all the degrees of greater or lesser extension where such a cycle can be envisaged) proceeding from its higher pole, which is Heaven, to its lower pole, which is Earth (or what represents these poles from a relative point of view if it is only a particular cycle) can be considered as starting from the least 'specified' form of all, the sphere, to end at that which is, on the contrary, the most 'fixed' of all, the cube;[11] and one could also say that the first of these two forms has an eminently 'dynamic' character and the second an eminently 'static' character, which also corresponds to the active and passive. Moreover, this representation can be related in a certain way to the foregoing by viewing the horizontal line in it

8. We shall see later that this perpendicular has still other meanings corresponding to different points of view; but for the moment we are only considering the geometrical representation of the complementarism of Heaven and Earth.

9. The figure formed by the vertical and horizontal so arranged is a well-known symbol even today in Anglo-Saxon Freemasonry, although it is one of those that so-called 'Latin' Freemasonry has not kept. In architectural symbolism generally, the vertical is represented by the perpendicular or plumb-line and the horizontal by the level. A similar placement of the two letters *alif* and *ba* in the Arabic alphabet also corresponds to the same symbolism.

10. *The Reign of Quantity and the Signs of the Times*, chap. 20.

11. In three-dimensional geometry the sphere naturally corresponds to the circle and the cube to the square.

as the trace of a plane surface (whose 'measured' area will be a square),[12] and the vertical line as the radius of a hemispherical surface which meets the terrestrial plane along the line of the horizon. And in fact it is at their periphery or their confines, that is, the horizon, that Heaven and Earth appear to meet; but it must be noted here that the reality symbolized by these appearances must be taken inversely, for according to that reality they are on the contrary united by the center,[13] or, if considered in the state of relative separation necessary that the Cosmos be able to develop between them, they communicate along the axis which passes through this center[14] and which at once unites and separates them, or, in other words, which measures the distance between Heaven and Earth, that is, the very extent of the Cosmos in the vertical direction which marks the hierarchy of the states of manifested existence while joining them one to the other across this multiplicity of states, which appear in this respect as so many rungs by which a being on the way of return toward the Principle can raise itself from Earth to Heaven.[15]

It is also said that Heaven, which envelops or embraces all things, presents to the Cosmos a 'ventral' or inward face, and that Earth, which supports all things, presents a 'dorsal' or outward, face.[16] This can easily be seen by an examination of the diagram below, in which Heaven and Earth are respectively represented by a concentric circle and a square (figure 8). It will be observed that this figure

12. This must be linked to the fact that in the symbols of certain grades of Masonry the spread of the compasses, whose arms correspond to the lateral sides of the triangle in figure 7, measures off a quarter circle whose chord is the side of the inscribed square.

13. It is through a similar application of the principle of inversion that the Terrestrial Paradise, which is also the point of communication between Heaven and Earth, appears at once to be situated at the extremity of the world from the 'outward' point of view, and at the very center of the world from the 'inward' point of view (cf. *The Reign of Quantity and the Signs of the Times*, chap. 23).

14. This axis is of course identical to the vertical radial in the preceding figure; but from this perspective, this radial corresponds not to Heaven itself but only to the direction in which the influence of Heaven acts upon Earth.

15. This is why, as we shall see later, the vertical axis is also the 'Way of Heaven' (*T'ien Tao*).

16. This assimilation would be immediately evident in a language like Arabic, where the front [abdomen] is *al-baṭin* and the interior *al-bāṭin*, the back *aẓ-ẓahr* and the exterior *aẓ-ẓāhir*.

reproduces the shape of Chinese coins, was originally the shape of certain ritual tablets:[17] the solid part between the circular periphery and the empty, square-shaped middle, on which the characters are inscribed, obviously corresponds to the Cosmos which contains the 'ten thousand beings',[18] and the fact that this area is bounded by two voids expresses symbolically that what is not between Heaven and Earth is for that very reason outside of manifestation altogether.[19] However, there is a point on which this figure can appear inexact and which corresponds to a defect that is necessarily inherent in every sensible representation: if one is aware only of the apparent positions of Heaven and Earth, or

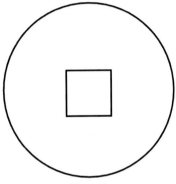

Figure 8

rather, of what represents them, it could seem that Heaven is on the outside and Earth on the inside; but the truth is that here again we must not forget to apply the analogy inversely. In reality, from every point of view, 'inwardness' belongs to Heaven and 'outwardness' to Earth, and we will meet with this again a little later. Besides, even taking the figure simply as it stands, we can see that because they are the outermost boundaries of the Cosmos, Heaven and Earth really have only one face with respect to the Cosmos, and that face is inward for Heaven and outward for Earth; and as for their other face, it must be said that this can exist only in relation to the common principle in which they are united and where every distinction of inward and outward disappears, along with every opposition and even every complementarity, leaving nothing behind but the 'Great Unity'.

17. On the symbolic value of coins in traditional civilizations in general, see *The Reign of Quantity and the Signs of the Times*, chap. 16.

18. It is hardly necessary to point out that the characters represent the names of the beings, and consequently represent them in an entirely natural way, especially in the case of an ideographic script such as that of the Chinese language.

19. The expression *T'ien hsia*, literally 'beneath Heaven', is generally used in Chinese to denote the totality of the Cosmos.

4

YIN AND *YANG*

IN ITS PROPERLY COSMOLOGICAL PART the Far-Eastern tradition attributes a capital importance to two principles, or if one prefers, to two 'categories', which it designates *yang* and *yin*. All that is active, positive, or masculine is *yang*; all that is passive, negative, or feminine is *yin*. These two categories are associated symbolically with light and darkness; in all things the light side is *yang*, the dark side is *yin*; but, as one can never be found without the other, they appear much more frequently as complementaries than as opposites.[1] This meaning of light and darkness figures literally in the determination of geographical sites;[2] and the more general meaning, where these terms *yang* and *yin* extend to the terms of every complementarity, has innumerable applications in all the traditional sciences.[3]

It is easy to understand from what has been said that *yang* is what proceeds from the nature of Heaven and *yin* what proceeds from the nature of Earth, since it is from this primary complementarism of

---

1. This distinction between light and darkness must therefore not be interpreted in terms of 'good' and 'evil' as is sometimes done elsewhere, for example in Mazdaism.

2. At first glance it may seem strange that the *yang* side should be the southern slope of a mountain, but the northern side of a valley or the northern bank of a river (the *yin* side naturally always opposite to this); but it is enough to consider the solar rays, which come from the south, to realize that in any case it is the illuminated side that is called *yang*.

3. Traditional Chinese medicine in particular is based more or less entirely on the distinction between *yang* and *yin*; every illness is due to a state of disequilibrium, that is, to an excess of one of these two in relation to the other; this must then be strengthened to re-establish the equilibrium, and in this way one reaches the very cause of the illness instead of being limited to treating more or less outward and superficial symptoms, as is the profane medicine of modern Westerners.

Heaven and Earth that all the other more or less particular complementarisms derive; and from this we can immediately see the reason
why these two terms have been assimilated to light and darkness.
Indeed, the *yang* aspect of beings corresponds to what in them is
'essential' or 'spiritual', and it is well known that Spirit is identified
with Light in the symbolism of all traditions; on the other hand, the
yin aspect of beings is that by which they relate to 'substance', and
this, by virtue of the 'unintelligibility' inherent in its indistinction or
its state of pure potentiality, can be properly defined as the dark root
of all existence. From this point of view we can also say, borrowing
Aristotelian and Scholastic terminology, that *yang* is everything that
is 'in act' and *yin* is everything that is 'in potency', or that every
being is *yang* to the extent it is 'in act' and yin to the extent it is 'in
potency', since both these aspects are necessarily found in every
manifested thing.

Heaven is entirely *yang* and Earth entirely *yin*, which amounts to
saying that Essence is pure act and Substance pure potency; but they
are so only in the pure state, insofar as they are the two poles of universal manifestation; and in all manifested things there is no *yang*
without *yin* and no *yin* without *yang*, for their nature partakes
simultaneously in both Heaven and Earth.[4] If we consider *yang* and
yin specifically as masculine and feminine elements it can be said
that by reason of this participation every being is in a certain sense
and to a certain degree 'androgynous' and that it is all the more so
insofar as these two elements are in equilibrium in it; the masculine
or feminine character of an individual being (or more precisely its
predominantly masculine or feminine character) can then be considered as resulting from the preponderance of one or the other. It
would naturally be inappropriate here to develop all the consequences that can be deduced from this observation, but a moment's
reflection is enough to perceive without difficulty their importance,
particularly for all the sciences that are concerned with the study of
individual man under the many points of view from which he can
be considered.

---

4. This is why, according to a Masonic formula, the initiate must be able to
'detect the light in the darkness [the *yang* in the *yin*] and the darkness in the light
[the *yin* in the *yang*].'

We saw above that Earth displays its 'dorsal' face and Heaven its 'ventral' face; this is why *yin* is 'outward' and *yang* 'inward'.[5] In other words, only terrestrial influences, which are *yin*, are sensible, while celestial influences, which are *yang*, elude the senses and can only be grasped by the intellectual faculties. This is one of the reasons why *yin* is generally mentioned before *yang* in traditional texts, a practice which may seem contrary to the hierarchic relationship that exists between the principles to which they correspond, that is, Heaven and Earth, insofar as they are the superior and inferior pole of manifestation. This reversal of the order of the two complementary terms is characteristic of a certain cosmological point of view, which is also that of the Hindu *Sāṅkhya*, where *Prakriti* figures similarly at the beginning of the enumeration of the *tattvas* and *Purusha* at the end. In fact, this point of view proceeds as it were 'from below upward', just as the construction of a building starts at its base and ends at the summit; it starts from what can be most immediately grasped and proceeds toward what is more hidden, that is, it goes from the outward to the inward, or from *yin* to *yang*; in this it is the inverse of the metaphysical point of view, which starting from the principle to proceed toward the consequences, goes on the contrary from the inward to the outward; and this inversion of directions shows clearly that these two points of view properly correspond to two different degrees of reality. Moreover, we have seen elsewhere that in the unfolding of the cosmogonic process, darkness, identified with chaos, is 'in the beginning', and light, which orders this chaos to draw from it the Cosmos, is 'after the darkness';[6] and this amounts again to saying that, in this respect, *yin* effectively comes before *yang*.[7]

---

5. Expressed in this way, the matter is immediately comprehensible for the Far-Eastern mentality; but we must recognize that without the explanations provided earlier on the subject the link thus established between these two propositions would be of a nature to singularly disconcert the special logic of Westerners.

6. *Perspectives on Initiation* chap. 46.

7. Something analogous to this can be found in the fact that, according to the symbolism of the sequence of the cycles, the lower states of existence appear to be antecedent in regard to the higher; this is why the Hindu tradition represents the *Asuras* as before the *Devas*, and describes the cosmogonic succession as occurring in the order *tamas, rajas, sattva*, thus as proceeding from darkness to light (see *The Symbolism of the Cross*, chap. 5, and also *The Esoterism of Dante*, chap. 6).

When *yang* and *yin* are considered separately, their linear symbols are what are called 'the two determinations' (*ül-i*), that is, the
solid line and the broken line, which are the elements forming the
trigrams and the hexagrams of the *I Ching*. These designs therefore
represent all the possible combinations of these two terms making
up the entirety of the manifested world. The first and last
hexagrams, *Ch'ien* and *K'un*,[8] are formed respectively of six solid
and six broken lines; they therefore represent the fullness of *yang*,
identified with Heaven, and *yin*, identified with Earth; and it is
between these two that all the other
hexagrams are located, *yang* and *yin*
combining in different proportions
and so corresponding to the unfolding of all manifestation. On the other
hand, when these two terms are
united they are represented by the
symbol called, for that reason, *yin-
yang* (figure 9),[9] that we have already
considered elsewhere from the view-

Figure 9

point where it represents the 'circle of individual destiny'.[10] In conformity with the symbolism of light and darkness, the light part of
the figure is *yang* and the dark part *yin*; and the central dots, dark in
the light part and light in the dark, recall that in reality *yang* and *yin*
are never found apart from each other. Insofar as the *yang* and the
yin are already differentiated while still being united (and it is for
this reason that the diagram is called *yin-yang*), it is the symbol of
the primordial 'Androgyne', since its elements are the masculine
and feminine principles; it is also, according to another and more

---

8. The same as the first and last of the eight trigrams (*kua*), which likewise consist of three solid and three broken lines; each hexagram is formed by the superpo-
sition of two trigrams, similar or different, giving sixty-four combinations in all.

9. This symbol is usually placed at the center of the eight trigrams, which are
arranged circularly around it.

10. *The Symbolism of the Cross*, chap. 22. In this respect, the *yin* part and the
yang part respectively represent the traces of the lower states and the reflection of
the higher states with respect to a given state of existence, such as the individual
human state, which agrees exactly with what we just noted about the relationship
between the succession of cycles and *yin* as anterior to *yang*.

general traditional symbolism, the 'World Egg', whose two halves, when they separate, become Heaven and Earth respectively.[11] From another point of view, the same figure considered as forming an indivisible whole,[12] which corresponds to the principial point of view, becomes the symbol of *T'ai Chi*, which appears thus as the synthesis of *yin* and *yang*, but on condition that it is clear that since this synthesis is the primal Unity, it is anterior to the differentiation of its elements, and therefore absolutely independent of them; in fact, there can be properly speaking no question of *yin* and *yang* except in relation to the manifested world, which as such proceeds entirely from the 'two determinations'. The two perspectives from which the symbol can be viewed are summed up in the following formula: 'The ten thousand beings are produced [*chao*] by *T'ai I* [which is equivalent to *T'ai Chi*] and modified [*hua*] by *yin-yang*,' for all beings come from the principial Unity,[13] but their modifications in 'becoming' are due to the reciprocal actions and reactions of the 'two determinations'.

11. Viewed as a plane surface, the figure corresponds to the diametrical section of the 'World Egg' at the level of that particular state of existence from which the totality of manifestation is envisaged.

12. The two halves are marked off from each other by a curved line that indicates an interpenetration of the two elements, whereas if they were divided by a diameter they might be seen as a mere juxtaposition. It is worth noting that this curved line is formed by two semi-circumferences, whose two radii are half that of the circumference forming the periphery of the whole figure, so that their total length is consequently equal to half that of the circumference; thus each of the two halves of the diagram is contained by a line equal in length to the line containing the whole diagram.

13. *T'ai I* is the *Tao* 'that has a name', which is 'the mother of the ten thousand beings' (*Tao Te Ching*, chap. 1). The *Tao* 'that has no name' is Non-Being, and the *Tao* 'that has a name' is Being: 'If we must give a name to the *Tao* [although it really cannot be named], it will always be called [as an approximate equivalent] the "Great Unity".'

5

THE DOUBLE SPIRAL

WE THINK IT WOULD NOT be without interest to make at least an apparent digression here regarding a symbol closely connected to the *yin-yang*. This is the double spiral (figure 10), which plays an extremely important role in the traditional art of the most diverse countries, particularly in that of ancient Greece.[1] As has been justly said, this double spiral, 'which can be regarded as the planar projection

Figure 10

of the two hemispheres of the Androgyne, offers an image of the alternating rhythm of evolution and involution, of birth and death, and in a word portrays manifestation in its double aspect.'[2]

Moreover, this figure can be envisaged both 'macrocosmically' and 'microcosmically', and because of their analogy it is always possible to go from the one of these two points of view to the other by means of the appropriate transposition; but it is particularly to the first that we will refer here, for it is in regard to the symbolism of the 'World Egg', to which we have already alluded in connection with the *yin-yang*, that the most remarkable relationships appear. From this point of view, the two spirals can be considered as the indication of a cosmic force acting in opposite directions in each of the two hemispheres, which, in their broadest application, are of course

---

1. In conformity with modern tendencies some naturally insist on seeing in this merely a 'decorative' or 'ornamental' motif; but they forget or do not know that all 'ornamentation' originally had a symbolic character even though its use may have continued by a kind of 'survival' in periods when this character was no longer understood.

2. Elie Lebasquais, 'Tradition hellènique et Art grec', in the December 1935 issue of *Études Traditionnelles*.

the two halves of the 'World Egg', the points around which the two spirals coil being the two poles.[3] It can be seen at once that this is closely related to the two directions of the rotation of the *swastika* (figure 11) since this essentially represents the same revolution of the world around its axis but viewed respectively now from one of the poles, now from the other;[4] and these two directions of rotation do indeed express the dual action of the cosmic force in question, a dual action which is at root the same thing as the duality of *yin* and *yang* under all their aspects.

It is easy to see that in the symbol of the *yin-yang* the two semi-circumferences that form the line dividing the light and dark sections of the figure correspond exactly to the two spi-

Figure 11

rals, and that their central points—dark in the light part, light in the dark—correspond to the two poles. This leads us back to the idea of the 'Androgyne', as we noted earlier; and let us once again note that the two principles *yin* and *yang* must in reality always be considered as complementaries, even if their respective actions in the different domains of manifestation appear outwardly to be contrary. We may thus speak either of the dual action of a single force, as we were just doing, or of two forces produced by its polarization and centered on the two poles, and producing in turn, by the actions and reactions that result from their very differentiation, the development of the virtualities enshrouded in the 'World Egg', a development that includes all the modifications of 'the ten thousand beings'.[5]

3. The double spiral is the principal element in certain talismans very widespread in Islamic countries; in one of its most complete forms, the two points in question are marked by stars representing the two poles; on a vertical median that corresponds to the plane dividing the two hemispheres we find, above and below the line connecting the two spirals to each other, the sun and moon; finally, at the four angles are four quadrangular figures corresponding to the four elements, which are thus identified with the four 'angles' (*arkān*) or foundations of the world.

4. Cf. *The Symbolism of the Cross*, chap. 10.

5. Those who like to find parallels with the profane sciences could, as a 'microcosmic' application, relate these figures to the phenomenon of 'caryokinesis', which is the initial stage of cell division; but of course, for our part, we attribute to all comparisons of this kind only a very relative importance.

It should be noted that these same two forces are also depicted in different though fundamentally equivalent ways in other traditional symbols, particularly by two helicoidal lines coiling in opposite directions around a vertical axis, as is seen for instance in certain forms of the *Brahma-danda* or Brahmanic staff, which is an image of the 'World Axis' and where this double coiling is related precisely to the two contrary orientations of the *swastika*; in the human being these two lines are the two *nādīs* or subtle currents, right and left, positive and negative (*idā* and *piṇgalā*).[6] Another identical figuration is the two serpents of the caduceus, which is linked moreover to the general symbolism of the serpent in its two opposite aspects;[7] and in this regard the double spiral can also be seen as representing a serpent coiled around itself in two opposite directions; this serpent is thus an *amphisbaena*,[8] whose two heads correspond to the two poles, and which by itself is equivalent to the two opposite serpents of the caduceus.[9]

All of this hardly takes us from a consideration of the 'World Egg', for in various traditions this is frequently related to the symbolism of the serpent; one will recall here the Egyptian *Kneph*, represented in the form of a serpent producing an egg from its mouth (an image of the production of manifestation by the Word),[10] and also, of

---

6. See *Man and His Becoming according to the Vedānta*, chap. 20. The 'World Axis' and the axis of the human being (represented corporeally by the vertebral column) are, by reason of their analogical correspondence, both designated by the term *Meru-ḍanḍa*.

7. Cf. *The Reign of Quantity and the Signs of the Times*, chap. 30.

8. Cf. *The King of the World*, chap. 3

9. To explain the formation of the caduceus it is said that Mercury saw two serpents fighting each other (a figure of chaos) and that he separated them (distinction of contraries) with a rod (determination of an axis along which chaos will be ordered in order to become the Cosmos) around which they coiled themselves (equilibrium of the two contrary forces acting symmetrically with respect to the 'World Axis'). It should also be noted that the caduceus (*kerukeion*, insignia of the heralds) is considered the characteristic attribute of the two complementary functions of Mercury or Hermes: on the one hand the Gods' interpreter and messenger, and on the other the 'psychopomp', conducting beings through their changes of state or their passage from one cycle of existence to another; these two functions correspond respectively to the descending and ascending currents represented by the two serpents.

10. See *Perspectives on Initiation*, chap. 47.

course, the Druidic symbol of the 'serpent's egg'.[11] On the other hand, the serpent is often portrayed as inhabiting the waters, as we see particularly in the case of the *Nāgas* in the Hindu tradition, and it is on these same waters that the 'World Egg' floats. Now these waters are the symbol of possibilities, and their development is represented by the spiral, hence the close association that sometimes exists between this last and the symbolism of the waters.[12]

If the 'World Egg' is thus in certain cases a 'serpent's egg', it is also sometimes a 'swan's egg';[13] we allude here particularly to the symbolism of *Hamsa*, the vehicle of *Brahmā* in the Hindu tradition.[14] Now it often happens, especially in Etruscan figures, that the double spiral is surmounted by a bird; this is obviously the same as *Hamsa*, the swan that broods over the *Brahmānda* upon the primordial Waters, and which is identified moreover with the 'spirit' or 'divine breath' (for *Hamsa* is also 'breath') which, according to the beginning of the Hebrew Genesis, 'was borne upon the face of the Waters.' What is no less remarkable is that, for the Greeks, from the egg of Leda, sired by Zeus in the form of a swan, come the Dioscuri Castor and Pollux, who symbolically correspond to the two hemispheres and thus to the two spirals we considered earlier, and who in consequence represent their differentiation in this 'swan's egg', that is to say, at root, the division of the 'World Egg' into its higher and lower halves.[15] We cannot elaborate further at

---

11. The serpent's egg is in fact represented by a fossil sea-urchin.

12. Attention was drawn to this association by Ananda K. Coomaraswamy in his study 'Angel and Titan' on the relationship between the *Devas* and *Asuras* ['Angel and Titan: An Essay in Vedic Ontology' (*Journal of the American Oriental Society*, LV, 1935, pp373–419)]. In Chinese art, the spiral occurs notably in the figurations of the 'double chaos' of the upper and lower waters (that is, of the supraformal and formal possibilities), often in conjunction with the symbolism of the Dragon (see *The Multiple States of the Being*, chap. 12).

13. The swan moreover recalls the serpent by the shape of its neck; it is thus in certain respects a combination of the symbols of the bird and the serpent, which often appear as opposed or complementary.

14. As concerns other traditions, it is also known that the symbolism of the swan was linked especially to that of the Hyperborean Apollo.

15. To make this signification more explicit, the Dioscuri are represented wearing caps of hemispherical shape.

present on the symbolism of the Dioscuri, which indeed is very complex, as is that of all similar couples formed of a mortal and an immortal, one often depicted as white and the other as black,[16] like the two hemispheres of which one is lit while the other remains in darkness. We will only say that this symbolism is basically very close to that of the *Devas* and *Asuras*,[17] whose opposition is equally bound up with the dual meaning of the serpent according to whether it moves in an upward or a downward direction around a vertical axis, or uncoils or coils on itself, as in the figure of the double spiral.[18]

In ancient symbols this double spiral is sometimes replaced by two sets of concentric circles, drawn around two points which again represent the poles; these are, at least in one of their more general meanings, the celestial and the infernal circles, the second being a kind of inverted reflection of the first,[19] and to which correspond precisely the *Devas* and the *Asuras*. In other words, they are the higher and the lower states relative to the human state, or the cycles antecedent and consequent with respect to the preceding cycle (which is ultimately only another way of expressing the same thing according to a 'sequential' symbolism); and this also corroborates an understanding of the *yin-yang* as a planar projection of the helix representing the multiple states of universal Existence.[20] The two symbols are equivalent, and the one can be considered a mere modification of the other; but the double spiral indicates in addition the continuity between the cycles; it can also be said that it represents

16. This is in particular the meaning of the names *Arjuna* and *Krishna*, which respectively represent *jīvātmā* and *Paramātmā*, or the 'ego' and the 'Self', the individuality and the personality, and which as such can be related to Earth and to Heaven.

17. This can be related to our remarks in an earlier note on the subject of the chain of cycles.

18. Cf. the study by Ananda K. Coomaraswamy already cited above. In the well-known symbolism of the 'churning of the sea', the *Devas* and the *Asuras* pull in opposite directions on the serpent coiled around the mountain, which represents the 'World Axis'.

19. We have already drawn attention to this connection in *The Esoterism of Dante*.

20. See *The Symbolism of the Cross*, chap. 22.

things in their 'dynamic' aspect, whereas the concentric circles represent them rather in their 'static' aspect.[21]

In speaking here of a 'dynamic' aspect, we naturally still have in mind the action of the dual cosmic force, and more particularly its relationship to the inverse and complementary phases of all manifestation, phases which are due, according to the Far-Eastern tradition, to the alternating predominance of *yin* and *yang*: 'evolution' or development, unfolding,[22] and 'involution' or envelopment, enfolding; or again, 'catabasis' or descending movement, and 'anabasis' or ascending movement, entry into the manifested, and return to the non-manifested.[23] This double 'spiration' (and one will notice the very significant kinship between the very name 'spiral' and that of *spiritus* or 'breath', of which we spoke earlier in connection with *Hamsa*) is the universal 'expiration' and 'inspiration' by which are produced, according to Taoist terminology, the 'condensations' and 'dissipations' resulting from the alternate action of *yin* and *yang*, or according to Hermetic terminology, the 'coagulations' and 'solutions'; for individual beings, these are births and deaths, what Aristotle calls *genesis* and *phthora*, 'generation' and 'corruption'; for

21. Of course, this does not prevent the circle from itself representing a 'dynamic' aspect in relation to the square, as we said above; consideration of the 'dynamic' and 'static' points of view always implies, by their very correlation, a question of relationship. If instead of considering the totality of universal manifestation one limits oneself to one world, that is, to the state corresponding to the plane of the figure considered as horizontal, its two halves would in every case represent the reflection of the higher states and the traces of the lower states in this world, as we have indicated earlier in connection with the *yin-yang*.

22. Needless to say, we take the word 'evolution' in its strictly etymological sense, which has nothing in common with its use in modern 'progressivist' theories.

23. It is strange, to say the least, that Léon Daudet chose the symbol of the double spiral as a 'schema of the ambience' (*Courriers des Pays-Bas*: see also the diagram in *Les Horreurs de la Guerre*, and his remarks on the 'ambience' in *Melancholia*); he envisages one of the two poles as a 'point of departure' and the other as a 'point of arrival', so that travel from one end of the spiral to the other can be regarded as involving a centrifugal movement on one side and a centripetal movement on the other, which corresponds to the 'evolutive' and 'involutive' phases; and what he calls 'ambience' is at root nothing but the 'astral light' of Paracelsus, which includes precisely both of the two inverse currents of the cosmic force that we are considering here.

worlds, they are what Hindu tradition calls the days and nights of *Brahmā*, like the *Kalpa* and the *Pralaya*; and at all degrees, in the 'macrocosmic' order as well as in the 'microcosmic' order, there are corresponding phases in every cycle of existence, for they are the very expression of the law that governs the sum total of universal manifestation.

6

SOLVE ET COAGULA

SINCE WE JUST ALLUDED to Hermetic 'coagulation' and 'solution', and even though we have already said quite a bit about this on different occasions, perhaps it will not be without profit to further clarify certain ideas that are rather directly related to what we have said on this point. Indeed, the formula *solve et coagula* is regarded as containing in a certain respect the whole secret of the 'Great Work' insofar as this reproduces the process of universal manifestation, with its two inverse phases that we have just noted. The term *solve* is sometimes represented by a sign depicting Heaven and the term *coagula* by a sign depicting Earth;[1] which is to say that they are likened to the actions of the ascending and descending currents of the cosmic force, or in other words to the respective actions of *yang* and *yin*. Every expansive force is *yang* and every contractive force is *yin*; the 'condensations' that give birth to individual composites therefore come from terrestrial influences, and the 'dissipations' that bring the elements of these composites back to their original principles come from the celestial influences. These are, so to speak, the effects of the respective attractions of Heaven and Earth, and it is thus that 'the ten thousand beings are modified by *yin* and *yang*' from the moment they appear in the manifested world until their return to the unmanifest.

---

1. We are alluding here to the symbolism of the signs of the 18th degree of Scottish Masonry and also to that of the rite of the 'calumet' among the North American Indians, which comprises three successive movements relating to Heaven, Earth, and Man respectively and which can be translated by the terms 'solution', 'coagulation', and 'assimilation'.

It must be carefully noted, moreover, that the order of these two terms depends upon the point of view one adopts, for in reality the two complementary phases to which they correspond are at once alternating and simultaneous, and their order depends as it were on the state taken as starting-point. If one starts from the state of non-manifestation and proceeds to manifestation (which is the point of view that can be called 'cosmogonic'),[2] it is naturally 'condensation' or 'coagulation' that will be first; 'dissipation' or 'solution' will come afterward as a movement of return toward the non-manifested, or at least toward what at any given level corresponds to it in a relative sense.[3] If on the contrary one starts from a given state of manifestation, one has first to envisage a tendency leading to the 'solution' of what is in that state; and a subsequent phase of 'coagulation' would be the return to another state of manifestation; moreover, we should add this 'solution' and 'coagulation' with regard to the antecedent state and the subsequent state respectively, can be perfectly simultaneous in reality.[4]

On the other hand, and this is even more important, things are inverted according to whether they are considered from the viewpoint of the Principle, or, on the contrary, from that of manifestation, as we just did, so that it could be said that what is *yin* on one side is *yang* on the other, and vice versa, although it is only very improperly that even a duality like that of *yin* and *yang* can be attributed to the Principle itself. Indeed, as we have already pointed out elsewhere,[5] it is the 'expiration' or movement of principial expansion which determines the 'coagulation' of the manifested, and the 'inspiration' or movement of principial contraction which determines its 'solution'; and it would be exactly the same if instead

---

2. The order of succession of the two phases regarded from this point of view shows again why *yin* here precedes *yang*.

3. This finds numerous applications in the domain of the traditional sciences; one of the lowest is the 'summoning' and 'dismissal' of 'wandering influences' at the beginning and end of a magical operation.

4. This is the 'death' to one state and 'birth' to another considered as the two opposite and inseparable faces of the same modification of the being (see *The Symbolism of the Cross*, chapter 22, and *Perspectives on Initiation*, chap. 26).

5. *Perspectives on Initiation*, chap. 47.

of using the symbolism of the two phases of respiration one were to use that of the double movement of the heart.

One can in any event avoid the impropriety of expression just mentioned by means of a simple remark: Heaven, as the 'positive' pole of manifestation, represents the Principle in a direct way in relation to manifestation,[6] whereas Earth, as the 'negative' pole, can only present an inverse image. The 'perspective' of manifestation will therefore quite naturally attribute to the Principle itself what really belongs to Heaven, and it is thus that the 'movement' of Heaven (movement in a purely symbolic sense, of course, since there is nothing spatial here) will be attributed in a certain way to the Principle although it is necessarily immutable. At root, it is more exact to speak as we did above of the respective attractions of Heaven and Earth, which work in opposite directions; every attraction produces a centripetal movement, thus a 'condensation' to which corresponds at the opposite pole a 'dissipation' determined by a centrifugal movement, so that total equilibrium is re-established, or rather maintained.[7] It follows that what is 'condensation' in relation to substance is on the contrary 'dissipation' in relation to essence, and that inversely, what is 'dissipation' in relation to substance is 'condensation' in relation to essence; consequently, every 'transmutation' in the Hermetic sense of the term will properly consist of 'dissolving' what was 'coagulated', and simultaneously 'coagulating' what was 'dissolved', these apparently inverse operations being in reality only the two complementary aspects of one and the same operation.

This is why the alchemists frequently say that 'the dissolution of the body is the fixation of the spirit,' and inversely, spirit and body being in the final analysis nothing else than the 'essential' and the 'substantial' aspect of the being; this can be understood as referring to the alternation of 'lives' and 'deaths' in the most general sense of these words, since this is what properly corresponds to the 'condensations' and 'dissipations' of Taoist tradition, so that one could say

6. That is why *T'ai Chi*, although higher than Heaven as well as Earth, and prior to their distinction, appears to us as the 'summit of Heaven'.

7. This can be compared with the considerations we laid out in *The Metaphysical Principles of the Infinitesimal Calculus*, chap. 17.

that the state which is life for the body is death for the spirit, and inversely;[8] and this is why to 'volatilize [or dissolve] the fixed and to fix [or coagulate] the volatile,' or to 'spiritualize the body and corporealize the spirit,'[9] is also said to be 'drawing the living from the dead and the dead from the living,' which is also a Koranic expression.[10] 'Transmutation' thus to one degree or another[11] implies a kind of reversal of ordinary relationships (by which we mean as viewed from the standpoint of the ordinary man), a reversal which is in reality a re-establishing of normal relationships; we will limit ourselves here to pointing out that this consideration of such a 'reversal' is particularly important from the standpoint of initiatic realization, without elaborating further, for this would require developments outside the framework of the present study.[12]

On the other hand, this double operation of 'coagulation' and 'solution' corresponds quite exactly to what Christian tradition calls the 'power of the keys'; this power is in fact also double, since it incorporates both the power to 'bind' and the power to 'loose'; now 'bind' is obviously the same thing as 'coagulate' and 'loose' the same thing as 'dissolve',[13] and comparison of different traditional symbols again confirms this correspondence as clearly as possible. It is well

---

8. According to the commentators on the *Tao Te Ching*, this alternation of states of life and death is the 'to-and-fro of the shuttle on the cosmic loom'; cf. *The Symbolism of the Cross*, chap. 14, where we also related other comparisons by the same commentators with breathing and with the lunar cycle.

9. In the same way it is said 'make the manifest hidden and hidden manifest.'

10. Koran VI:95. On the alternation of lives and deaths and the final return to the Principle see II:28.

11. To understand the reasons for this restriction, one has only to refer to what we said in *Perspectives on Initiation*, chap. 42.

12. At the highest level this 'reversal' is closely connected to what in Kabbalistic symbolism is called the 'shifting of lights' and also to the saying which Islamic tradition attributes to the *awliyā*: 'Our bodies are our spirits and our spirits our bodies' (*asjāmnā arwāḥnā, wa arwāḥnā ajsāmnā*). On the other hand, this 'reversal' also means that in the spiritual order it is the 'inward' that encloses the 'outward', which justifies what we said earlier about the relationships between Heaven and Earth.

13. In Latin, moreover, there is the expression *potestas ligandi et solvendi* [the power to bind and loose]. 'Ligature' in the literal sense is found in the magical use of knots, which has its counterpart in the usage of the points in the 'dissolution' process.

known that the power in question is usually represented in the form of two keys, one of gold and the other of silver, which refer respectively to the spiritual authority and the temporal power, or to the priestly function and the royal function, and also, from the initiatic point of view, to the 'greater mysteries' and the 'lesser mysteries' (and it is in this last respect that among the ancient Romans they were one of the attributes of Janus).[14] Alchemically, they refer to analogous operations accomplished at two different levels, respectively the 'whitening', which corresponds to the 'lesser mysteries', and the 'reddening', which corresponds to the 'greater mysteries'. These two keys, which in the language of Dante are those to the 'Celestial Paradise' and to the 'Terrestrial Paradise', are crossed in a manner reminiscent of the *swastika*. In

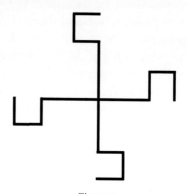

Figure 12

such a case, each of the two keys must be considered to possess the order to which it relates the double power of 'opening' and of 'closing', or of 'binding' and of 'loosing';[15] but there exists another more complete representation where for each of the two orders the two inverse powers are distinctly represented by two opposed keys. This figure is known as the 'claviger' *swastika* precisely because each of its four arms is made from a key (figure 12);[16] this gives us two keys

14. See *Spiritual Authority and Temporal Power*, chaps. 5 and 8, and also, on the relationship of the 'greater mysteries' and 'lesser mysteries' with 'sacerdotal initiation' and 'royal initiation' respectively, *Perspectives on Initiation*, chaps. 39 and 40.

15. Even so, it can be said that in a certain sense the power to 'bind' predominates in the key corresponding to the temporal, and the power to 'loose' in the key corresponding to the spiritual, for the temporal and the spiritual are *yin* and *yang* with respect to each other; this can be justified even outwardly when we speak of 'constraint' in the first domain and of 'freedom' in the second.

16. Many variants of this figure exist; the figure we reproduce here is found beside an ordinary *swastika* on an Etruscan vase in the Louvre Museum. One can see a Christian representation similar to the 'claviger' *swastika* in Mgr Devoucoux's introduction to *Histoire de l'antique cité d' Autun*, by Canon Edme Thomas, p xlvi.

opposed along a vertical axis, and two others along a horizontal axis.[17] With respect to the annual cycle, whose close connection with the symbolism of Janus is well known, the first of these two axes is a solstitial axis and the second an equinoctial axis;[18] here, the vertical or solstitial axis corresponds to the priestly function and the horizontal or equinoctial axis to the royal function.[19]

The connection between this symbol and the double spiral is confirmed by another form of the *swastika* which has curved arms with the appearance of two crossed S's; the double spiral can of course be identified either with its vertical or its horizontal part. It is true that the double spiral is usually arranged horizontally in order to bring out the complementary and as it were symmetrical character of the two currents of the cosmic force,[20] but on the other hand the curved line that is its equivalent in the *yin-yang* is on the contrary generally arranged vertically; thus, depending on the case, one may choose to consider either of these two positions, both of which are united in the curved-arm *swastika*, where they then correspond respectively to the two domains in which the 'power of the keys' is exercised.[21]

17. Strictly speaking, we should say an axis relatively vertical and an axis relatively horizontal with respect to each other, for the *swastika* itself is regarded as drawn on a horizontal plane (see *The Symbolism of the Cross*, chap. 10). — The key is essentially an 'axial' symbol, as is the staff or sceptre which in certain representations of Janus is substituted for the one of the two keys that corresponds to the temporal power or to the 'lesser mysteries'.

18. In the most common representations of Janus (*Janus Bifrons*) the two faces correspond (among other meanings) to the two solstices; but there are also, though more rarely, representations of Janus with four faces (*Janus Quadrifrons*), corresponding to the two solstices and the two equinoxes together, and rather curiously resembling the *Brahmā Chaturmukha* of Hindu tradition.

19. Let us note in passing that certain consequences can be drawn from this concerning the significance of the predominance attributed to the solstices in certain traditional forms and to the equinoxes in certain others, particularly for the purpose of fixing the start of the year; we only say that the solstitial point of view has in any event a more 'primordial' character than the equinoctial point of view.

20. This symmetry in the case of the two serpents of the caduceus is also particularly clear.

21. Medicine, which for the ancients belonged to the 'sacerdotal art', accordingly corresponds to a vertical position of the double spiral, insofar as it puts into action, as we said above, the respective forces of *yang* and *yin*. This vertical double

Another parallel to this 'power of the keys' is the double power of the *vajra* in the Hindu and Tibetan traditions.[22] This is widely known to be a symbol of the thunderbolt,[23] and its two extremities, composed of spokes in the shape of flames, correspond to the two opposed aspects of the power represented by the thunderbolt: generation and destruction, life and death.[24] If we compare the *vajra* to the 'World Axis', these two extremities correspond to the two poles, and thus to the two solstices;[25] it must then be aligned vertically, which agrees moreover with its character as a masculine symbol[26] as well as with the fact that it is essentially a sacerdotal attribute.[27] In a vertical position, then, the *vajra* represents the 'Middle Way', which is also, as we shall later see, the 'Way of Heaven'; but it can also be inclined to one side or the other, and then those two positions correspond to the two Tantric 'paths' of the right and of the left

---

spiral is represented by the serpent coiled in an 'S' about the staff of Asklepius, and here is represented alone in order to express that medicine uses only the 'benefic' aspect of the cosmic force. — It should be noted that the term 'spagyry', which is the designation for Hermetic medicine, formally expresses by its composition the double operation of 'solution' and 'coagulation'; the exercise of traditional medicine is thus the application in a particular order of the 'power of the keys'.

22. *Vajra* is the Sanskrit word; the Tibetan form is *dorje*.

23. It is both 'thunderbolt' and 'diamond' by a double acceptation of the same word, and is an 'axial' symbol in both of these meanings.

24. Certain double-edged weapons also represent this, for example the double axe in the symbolism of ancient Greece, whose meaning can be compared to that of the caduceus. On the other hand, the thunderbolt was represented by the hammer of Thor in Scandinavian tradition, to which can be compared the Master's mallet in Masonic symbolism. This is therefore still an equivalent of the *vajra* and, like it, has the double power of bringing life and death, as is shown by its role in initiatic consecration on the one hand and on the other in the legend of Hiram.

25. In the spatial symbolism of the annual cycle the solstices correspond to the North (winter) and the South (summer), while the two equinoxes correspond to the East (spring) and to the West (autumn); these relationships have a particularly great ritual importance in the Far-Eastern tradition.

26. Its feminine complement in the Hindu tradition is the conch (*shankha*), and in the Tibetan tradition, the ritual hand-bell (*dilbu*), on which there is often a feminine figure representing *Prajñā-pāramitā* or 'transcendent Wisdom', of which it is the symbol, while the *vajra* is that of the 'Method' or the 'Way'.

27. Lamas hold the *vajra* in their right hand and the hand-bell in their left; these two ritual objects must never be separated.

(*dakshina-mārga* and *yāma-mārga*), and this 'right' and 'left' can be related to the equinoctial points, just as 'up' and 'down' can be related to the solstitial points.[28] There is obviously much more to say about all this, but in order not to stray too far from our subject we must be satisfied with these few indications; and we will conclude the above remarks by saying that the power of the *vajra*, or the 'power of the keys' which is fundamentally identical with it since it implies the control and application of the cosmic forces in their double aspect of *yin* and *yang*, amounts in the end to nothing other than the very power of commanding life and death.[29]

28. One sometimes finds in Tibetan symbolism a figure consisting of two crossed *vajras*, which is obviously an equivalent of the *swastika*; the four ends then correspond exactly to the four keys of the 'claviger' *swastika*.

29. In ancient manuscripts originating from Operative Masonry there is mention with no further explanation of a certain *faculty of abrac*; this enigmatic word *abrac*, which has elicited different more or less fantastic interpretations and which is obviously distorted, seems indeed to have really signified the 'thunderbolt' or 'flash of lightning' (in Hebrew, *ha-baraq*, in Arabic, *al-barq*), so that here too we have the power of the *vajra*. From all of this it is easy to understand which symbolism has led the most diverse peoples to often regard the power provoking storms as a kind of consequence of initiation.

7

QUESTIONS
OF ORIENTATION

IN THE PRIMORDIAL AGE man was in perfect equilibrium with himself as to the complementarism of *yin* and *yang*; on the other hand, he was *yin* or passive in relation to the Principle alone, and *yang* or active in relation to the Cosmos or to the totality of manifested things; he therefore naturally turned toward the North, which is *yin*,[1] as toward his proper complement. In contrast, as a result of the spiritual degeneration that corresponds to the descending course of the cycle, the man of later ages has become *yin* in relation to the Cosmos; he must therefore turn to the South, which is *yang*, to receive from it the influences of the principle complementary to that which has become predominant in him and to re-establish as far as possible the equilibrium between *yin* and *yang*. The first of these two orientations can be called 'polar' while the second is properly 'solar'; in the first case, facing the pole star or 'summit of heaven', man has the East on his right and the West on his left; in the second case, facing the Sun at its meridian, he has the East on his left and the West on his right; and this provides an explanation for a peculiarity in the Far-Eastern tradition that might seem quite strange to those who do not know the reason for it.[2]

---

1. This is why in Masonic symbolism the Lodge is not to have any window opening onto the North whence the solar light never comes, whereas it does have them on the other three sides, which correspond to the three 'stations' of the sun.

2. In Chinese maps and plans the South is placed at the top and the North at the bottom, the East on the left and the West on the right, in conformity with the second orientation; this usage is moreover not as exceptional as one might suppose, for it also existed among the ancient Romans and even survived during part of the Western Middle Ages.

In China the side generally given pre-eminence is the left; we say 'generally', for this was not always so during the course of history. At the time of the historian Ssu-ma Ch'ien (that is, in the second century BC) the right seems to have been preponderant over the left, at least as concerns the hierarchy of official functions;[3] it seems that there was at that time, at least in this respect, a sort of attempt to 'return to the origins', which doubtless must have coincided with a change of dynasty, for such changes in the human order have always corresponded traditionally with certain modifications in the cosmic order itself.[4] But at an earlier period, although assuredly far removed from the primordial age, it was the left that predominated, as this passage from Lao Tzu indicates: 'In favorable [or well-omened] affairs, the left is placed uppermost, but in ill-omened affairs, the right is placed above.'[5] It was also said, around the same period, that 'Humanity is the right, the Way is the left,'[6] which obviously implies an inferiority of right with respect to left; relative to each other, the left corresponded to *yang* and right to *yin*.

Now that this is a direct consequence of the orientation toward the South is proved by a treatise attributed to Chuang Tzu, who is thought to have lived in the seventh century BC, in which is written: 'Spring gives birth [to beings] on the left, autumn destroys on the right, summer gives increase in front, winter lays by behind.' According to the generally admitted correspondence between the seasons and the cardinal points, spring corresponds to the East and autumn to the West, summer to the South and winter to the North;[7] thus here the South is indeed in front and the North behind, the

---

3. The 'counselor on the right' (*iu-t'san*) had at that time a more important role than the 'counselor on the left' (*tso-t'san*).

4. The succession of the dynasties, for example, corresponds to a succession of the elements in a specific order, the elements themselves being related to the seasons and to the cardinal points.

5. *Tao Te Ching*, chap. 31.

6. *Li Chi*.

7. This correspondence, which is in strict conformity with the nature of things, is common to all traditions; it is therefore incomprehensible why the moderns who occupy themselves with symbolism have so often substituted other correspondences that are purely fanciful and altogether unjustified. To give just one example, the table of quaternaries found at the end of Oswald Wirth's *Livre de l'Apprenti* does indeed relate summer to the South and winter to the North, but relates spring

East to the left and the West to the right.[8] Naturally, when one orients on the contrary toward the North, left and right become inverted, as do front and rear; but in the end, the side that has preeminence, whether it be the left or the right, is always and invariably the East. It is this that really matters, for it shows that the Far-Eastern tradition is fundamentally in perfect accord with all the other traditional doctrines, which always view the East as the 'luminous side' (*yang*) and the West as the 'dark side' (*yin*). The change in the respective meanings of the right and the left, being conditioned by a change of orientation, is therefore perfectly logical and implies absolutely no contradiction.[9]

These questions of orientation are moreover very complex, for not only is it always necessary to guard against confusing different correspondences, but it can also happen that in one and the same correspondence the right or the left will take precedence according to different points of view. This is very clearly demonstrated in a text such as the following:

> The Way of Heaven prefers the right; Sun and Moon move toward the West. The Way of Earth prefers the left; water flows toward the East. Both alike are above [that is to say, both sides have a claim to pre-eminence].[10]

This passage is particularly interesting, first because it affirms (for whatever reasons, which must be taken as mere 'illustrations' drawn

---

to the West and autumn to the East; and there are other correspondences, particularly relating to the ages of human life, that are muddled almost inextricably.

8. This can also be compared with the following text from the *I Ching*: 'The Sage faces toward the South and listens to the echo of what is under Heaven [that is, of the Cosmos]; it illumines and governs him.'

9. There can be still other modes of orientation than those we have just noted, and these will naturally entail different adaptations, but it is always easy to make them agree. Thus in India, if the right-hand side (*dakshina*) is the South, this is because orientation is taken by facing the Sun at its rising, that is, by turning to the East; but this present mode of orientation in no way precludes recognition of the primordiality of the 'polar' orientation, that is, toward the North, which is designated as the highest point (*uttara*).

10. *Chou Li.*

from sensible appearances) that the pre-eminence of the right is associated with the 'Way of Heaven' and that of the left with the 'Way of Earth'; now the first is necessarily superior to the second, and one could say it is because men have lost sight of the 'Way of Heaven' that they have come to conform to the 'Way of Earth', which clearly marks the difference between the primordial age and the later ages of spiritual degeneration. Next, one can see here the indication of an inverse relationship between the movement of Heaven and the movement of Earth,[11] which is in strict conformity to the general law of analogy; and it is always so when there are two terms that oppose one another in such a way that one of them is a reflection of the other, a reflection that is inverted as the image of an object in a mirror is inverted in relation to the object itself, so that the right of the image corresponds to the left of the object and vice versa.[12]

We will add in this connection a remark that, while appearing rather simple in itself, is nevertheless far from being unimportant; it is that, especially when it is a question of right and left, the greatest care must always be taken to state precisely the perspective from which the opposites are being envisaged; thus, when one speaks of the right and left of a symbolic figure, does one mean the right and left of the figure itself or the right and left of a spectator looking at it from the front? Either could be the case in fact; with a human figure or that of some other living being there is hardly any doubt as to which side should be called its right and left, but it is no longer the same for other objects, for a geometrical figure, for example, or a monument, and here right and left are normally determined by the point of view of the observer;[13] but this is not necessarily always the

---

11. Let us recall once more that 'movement' here is only a purely symbolic description.

12. Moreover, the same applies in the case of two people facing each other, which explains the saying: 'You will worship your right side, which is the left of your brother [the side of his heart]' (*Fan-k'ua Tu*, quoted by Matgioi, *La Voie rationnelle*, chap. 7).

13. Thus in the Kabbalistic figure of the 'sephirotic tree', the 'right-hand column' and the 'left-hand column' are respectively to one's right and to one's left as one looks at the figure.

case, and it can also happen that sometimes a left and right are attributed to an object or figure taken in itself, which will correspond to a point of view that is naturally the inverse of that of the spectator.[14] Without explaining in each case what it is, one may be led to rather serious errors in this regard.[15]

Another question related to that of orientation concerns the direction of the ritual 'circumambulations' in different traditional

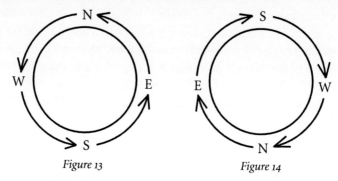

Figure 13   Figure 14

forms; it is easy to see that this direction is determined either by 'polar' or 'solar' orientation in the sense we gave these words above. If we consider the adjacent figures,[16] the first direction is that of the

14. For example, Plutarch relates that 'the Egyptians think of the East as the front of the world, the North as its right side and the South as its left' (*Isis and Osiris*, chap. 32). In spite of appearances, this coincides exactly with the Hindu designation of the South as the 'right side', for it is easy to envisage the left side of the world as on the right of the person observing it, and vice versa.

15. It is from this that derive, for example, the divergences in Masonic symbolism on the subject of the respective locations of the two pillars placed at the entrance to the Temple of Jerusalem; but the question is easy enough to resolve by referring directly to the biblical texts, provided we know that in Hebrew 'right' always means the South, and 'left' the North, which implies that orientation is made, as in India, by turning toward the East; moreover, this very same method of orientation was also that used in the West by the builders of the Middle Ages to determine the orientation of churches.

16. The cross drawn inside a circle, which we shall have to speak of again further on, here marks the direction of the four cardinal points; in accordance with what was said above, the North is placed at the top in the first diagram and the South in the second.

stars turning about the pole when one looks North (figure 13); on the other hand, the second direction is that of the Sun's apparent movement for an observer facing South (figure 14). The circumambulation is accomplished in the first case with the center continually on the left, and on the right in the second (which in Sanskrit is called *pradakshiṇa*); this last mode is the one used, in particular, in the Hindu and Tibetan traditions, while the other is found primarily in the Islamic tradition.[17]

Also connected with this difference in direction is the question of advancing with the right foot or the left foot first in ritual procession. Still considering the same figures, it is easy to see that the foot first advanced is necessarily that opposite the side turned toward the center of the circumambulation, that is, the right foot in the first case (figure 13) and the left foot in the second (figure 14); and this sequence is generally observed, even when it is not strictly speaking a question of circumambulation, as marking the respective predominance of the 'polar' or the 'solar' point of view, either in a particular traditional form, or sometimes even for different periods during the existence of one and the same traditional form.[18]

Thus, all these matters are far from being limited to more or less insignificant details, as those who understand nothing of either symbolism or rites might think; on the contrary, they are bound up with a whole body of notions of great importance in all traditions, and many other examples could be given. In connection with orientation one could also treat of questions such as its relationships

17. It is perhaps not without interest to note that the direction of these circumambulations—respectively from right to left (figure 13) and from left to right (figure 14)—also corresponds to the direction of writing in the sacred languages of these same traditional forms. In Masonry in its present form, the direction of the circumambulations is 'solar', but it seems on the contrary first to have been 'polar' in the ancient Operative ritual, in which the 'throne of Solomon' was placed, not in the East, but in the West, so as to permit its occupant to 'behold the Sun at its rising.'

18. The reversal in this sequence that has occurred in certain Masonic rites is all the more strange for its manifest disagreement with the direction of the circumambulations; the information we have just supplied clearly provides the correct rule to be observed in all cases.

to the course of the annual cycle[19] and to the symbolism of the 'zodiacal doors'; one would also find there an application of the inversion which we spoke of above in its relation with the 'celestial' and 'terrestrial' orders; but such considerations would constitute too long a digression, and they will doubtless find a better place in other studies.[20]

19. An example of this course being represented in the form of a circumambulation will be found in our discussion of the *Ming T'ang* further on.

20. On the qualitative character of the directions of space, which is the very principle on which the traditional importance of orientation rests, and on the relationship between the spatial and temporal determinations, see also the explanations we gave in *The Reign of Quantity and the Signs of the Times*, chaps. 4 and 5.

8

CELESTIAL AND TERRESTRIAL NUMBERS

THE DUALITY OF *yang* and *yin* is also found in numbers; according to the *I Ching*, the odd numbers correspond to *yang*, that is, they are masculine or active, and the even numbers correspond to *yin*, that is, they are feminine or passive. There is nothing here that is particular to the Far-Eastern tradition, for this correspondence conforms to what all traditional doctrines teach; in the West it was familiar especially to Pythagorism, and some who imagine it to be a concept proper to this doctrine might be very surprised to learn that exactly the same correspondences are found in the Far East, obviously without the possibility of the least 'borrowing' on either side, simply because this is a truth that must be equally recognized wherever the traditional science of numbers exists.

Because they are *yang*, odd numbers may be called 'celestial', and even numbers, because they are *yin*, may be called 'terrestrial'; but beyond this altogether general consideration there are certain numbers that are attributed especially to Heaven and to Earth, and this calls for other explanations. To begin with, it is the first two odd and even numbers respectively that are regarded as the numbers proper to Heaven and to Earth, or as the expression of their very nature, and this can be easily understood, for by virtue of the primacy each has in its own order, all the other numbers are in a way derived from them and occupy only a second rank in relation to them in their respective series; it is these, then, that so to speak represent *yang* and *yin* to the highest degree, or, what amounts to the same thing, express the celestial nature and the terrestrial most purely. Now, what must be borne in mind here is that unity, being properly the principle of number, cannot itself be counted as a number; in reality, what it represents can only be anterior to the distinction of Heaven and Earth, and we have already seen that it corresponds to the common principle of both of them, namely *T'ai Chi*, the Being that is identical to metaphysical Unity itself. Thus, while 2 is the first even number, it is 3 and not 1 that is considered the first odd number; consequently, 2 is the number of Earth and 3 the number of Heaven; but then, since 2 comes before 3 in the series of numbers, Earth appears to be before Heaven just as *yin* appears before *yang*. We find thus in these numerical correspondences another expression, fundamentally equivalent, of the same cosmological point of view that we spoke of earlier in connection with *yin* and *yang*.

What may seem more difficult to explain is that other numbers are also attributed to Heaven and Earth, and these produce, at least in appearance, a sort of inversion; indeed, it is 5, an odd number, that is attributed to Earth, and 6, an even number, that is attributed to Heaven. Here again there are two consecutive numbers in the series of numbers, the first of which corresponds to Earth and the second to Heaven; but apart from this one characteristic, common to the pairs of numbers 2 and 3 on the one hand, and to 5 and 6 on the other, how can it be that an odd or *yang* number is associated with Earth and an even or *yin* number is associated with Heaven? Some have spoken—and with good reason—of a 'hierogamic'[1] exchange between the attributes of the two complementary principles;[2] moreover, this is not an isolated or exceptional case and many

---

1. This term is formed from the Greek *hieros gamos*, or 'sacred marriage'. ED.

2. Marcel Granet, *La Pensée chinoise*, pp154–5 and 198–9. As we have already pointed out elsewhere (*The Reign of Quantity and the Signs of the Times*, chap. 5), this book contains a wealth of interesting information, and the chapter devoted to numbers is particularly important; but one must be careful to consult it strictly from a 'documentary' point of view and to disregard the author's 'sociological' interpretations, which generally reverse the true relationships of things, for it was not the cosmic order that was conceived on the model of social institutions, as Granet believes, but, quite to the contrary, these institutions were themselves established on the basis of correspondence with the cosmic order.

other similar examples could be found in traditional symbolism.[3] In reality, it would be necessary to generalize even further, for one cannot properly speak of 'hierogamy' except when the two complementary terms are expressly envisaged as masculine and feminine in relation to one another, as they are here; but one also finds something similar in cases where the complementarism assumes quite different aspects. We have already noted this elsewhere in connection with time and space and the symbols associated with them in the traditions of nomadic and sedentary peoples respectively.[4] It is obvious that in this case, where a temporal term and a spatial term are viewed as complementary, the relationship between them cannot be assimilated to that between the masculine and feminine; but it is true nonetheless that this complementarism, like every other, is related in a certain way to that between Heaven and Earth, for time is linked with Heaven through the notion of cycles, whose basis is essentially astronomical, and space with the Earth insofar as, in the order of sensible appearances, the terrestrial surface represents measurable extension. It must certainly not be concluded from this correspondence that all complementarisms can be reduced to a single type, and that is why it would be a mistake to speak of 'hierogamy' in a case like that we just mentioned; what must be said is that all complementarities, of whatever type, have their principle in the first of all dualities, which is that of universal Essence and universal Substance, or in the symbolic language of the Far-Eastern tradition, that of Heaven and Earth.

What must be realized if we are to accurately understand the different meaning of the two pairs of numbers attributed to Heaven and Earth is that an exchange like the one just now in question can only occur when the two complementary terms are considered in relation to each other, or more particularly as united to each other if it is a case of 'hierogamy' properly speaking, and not be taken in themselves and separately from each other. From this it results that whereas 2 and 3 represent Earth and Heaven in themselves and in

---

3. We will meet with an example of this kind later, again from the Far-Eastern tradition, on the subject of the square and the compasses.

4. *The Reign of Quantity and the Signs of the Times,* chap. 21.

their own nature, 5 and 6 are Earth and Heaven in their reciprocal action and reaction, and therefore from the point of view of the manifestation which is the product of this action and reaction. This is expressed very clearly by a text such as this: '5 and 6, this is the central union [*chung ho*, that is, the union at their center][5] of Heaven and Earth.'[6] This becomes even more apparent from the very constitution of the numbers 5 and 6, which are both formed from 2 and 3, but in different ways, by addition in the first case (2 + 3 = 5) and by multiplication in the second (2 x 3 = 6); moreover, this is why 5 and 6, both born from the union of even and odd, are very commonly regarded in the symbolism of different traditions as each having an essentially 'conjunctive' character.[7] To carry our explanation further, it must also be asked why there is addition in the case of Earth envisaged in its union with Heaven, and multiplication in the case of Heaven considered inversely in its union with Earth. This is because while each of the two principles receives through the union the influence of the other, which joins in a way with its nature, they nonetheless receive it differently. By the action of Heaven on Earth, the celestial number 3 is simply added to the terrestrial number 2, for that action is properly 'non-acting' and is what can be called an 'action of presence'; and by the reaction of Earth with respect to Heaven, the terrestrial number 2 multiplies the celestial number 3, because the potentiality of substance is the very root of multiplicity.[8]

5. What we said earlier will be remembered here, that Heaven and Earth can be effectively joined only at the center.

6. *Ch'ien Han-chu.*

7. For the Pythagoreans, 5 was the 'nuptial number' insofar as it was the sum of the first even, or feminine, number and the first odd, or masculine, number; as for the 'conjunctive' character of the number 6, we have only to think of the meaning of the letter *waw* [which has the numerical value of 6] in Hebrew and Arabic, or of the figure of the 'Seal of Solomon', which corresponds geometrically to this number. On the symbolism of the numbers 5 and 6 see also *The Symbolism of the Cross*, chap. 28.

8. The interchanging of even and odd is the natural result of this very mode of forming the two numbers, for the sum of an even number and an odd number will always be odd, while the product of an even number and an odd number is necessarily even. The sum of two numbers can only be even when they are both either even or odd; but if their product is to be odd, the two factors must each be odd.

It can also be said that whereas 2 and 3 express the very nature of Earth and Heaven, 5 and 6 express only their 'measure', which amounts to saying that it is rather from the viewpoint of manifestation that they are then considered, and not in themselves; for as we have explained elsewhere,[9] the very notion of 'measure' is directly related to manifestation. Heaven and Earth in themselves are in no way measurable since they do not belong to the domain of manifestation; one can speak of 'measure' only in reference to the determinations whereby they appear to the view of manifested beings,[10] which are what can be called celestial and terrestrial influences, expressed by the respective actions of *yang* and *yin*. To understand more precisely how this notion of 'measure' is applied, we must return to a consideration of the geometrical forms which symbolize the two principles and which are, as we saw earlier, the circle for Heaven and the square for Earth;[11] rectilinear forms, of which the square is the prototype, are measured by 5 and its multiples, and similarly, circular forms are measured by 6 and its multiples. In speaking of the multiples of these two numbers, we principally have in mind the first of these multiples, that is, the double of each, or 10 and 12 respectively. Indeed, the natural measure of straight lines is by decimal division and that of circular lines by duodecimal division, and in this can be seen the reason why the numbers 10 and 12 are the base for the principal systems of numeration, systems which are sometimes employed concurrently, as is precisely the case in China, because in reality they have different applications, so that their coexistence in one and the same traditional form has absolutely nothing arbitrary or superfluous about it.[12]

9. *The Reign of Quantity and the Signs of the Times*, chap. 3.

10. This 'view' must be understood as both in the sensible order and the intellectual order, according to whether it is a question of terrestrial influences, which are 'external', or of celestial influences, which are 'internal', as we have already explained above.

11. It is here that the compasses and square appear as instruments of measure from the 'celestial' and 'terrestrial' points of view respectively (that is, with respect to the corresponding influences). We shall speak of these below.

12. Here another exchange occurs in that, in some cases, the number 10 is attributed to Heaven and the number 12 to Earth, as if to mark once again their interdependence with regard to manifestation or to the cosmic order properly

To end these remarks we shall also point out the importance attached to the number 11 insofar as it is the sum of 5 and 6, which makes it the symbol of the 'central union of Heaven and Earth' mentioned above, and consequently 'the number that establishes the perfection [*cheng*][13] of the Way of Heaven and of Earth.'[14] The importance of the number 11 as well as of its multiples is yet another common element in the most diverse traditional doctrines, as we have already noted on another occasion,[15] although for reasons which are not very clear it goes largely unnoticed by those moderns who claim to study the symbolism of numbers.[16] These considerations on numbers could be developed almost indefinitely, but so far we have only considered Heaven and Earth, which are the first two terms of the Great Triad, and it is time now to pass on to a consideration of the third term of this triad, that is, Man.

---

speaking, both as to spatial and to temporal relationships; but we will not stress any further this point which would lead us far from our subject. We will only note as a particular example of this exchange that in Chinese tradition the days are counted in decimal periods and the months in duodecimal periods; now, ten days are 'ten suns', and twelve months are 'twelve moons', so that the numbers 10 and 12 are thus related, respectively, to the sun, which is *yang* or masculine and corresponds to Heaven, fire, and the South, and to the moon, which is *yin* or feminine and corresponds to Earth, water, and the North.

13. In the *I Ching* the word *cheng* is the final term in the tetragrammatic formula of *Wen Wang* (see Matgioi, *La Voie métaphysique*, chap. 5).

14. *Ch'ien Han-chu*.

15. See *The Esoterism of Dante*, chap. 7.

16. In the Hermetic and the Kabbalistic traditions 11 is the synthesis of the 'microcosm' and the 'macrocosm', represented respectively by the numbers 5 and 6, which also correspond, in another application, to individual man and to 'Universal Man' (or to terrestrial man and celestial man, to tie this to the terminology of the Far-Eastern tradition). — Since we have spoken of the numbers 10 and 12, we will also mention the importance from the Kabbalistic point of view of their sum 22 (two times 11, or its first multiple), which is known to be the number of letters in the Hebrew alphabet.

9

THE SON OF
HEAVEN AND EARTH

'HEAVEN IS HIS FATHER, Earth his mother'; this is the initiatic formula, always identical in the most diverse circumstances of time or place,[1] which determines the relationship of Man with the other two terms of the Great Triad, defining him as 'Son of Heaven and Earth'. It is already evident, by the very fact this is an initiatic formula, that the being to which it is applied in its fullness is much less the ordinary man such as he is in the conditions of our world than the 'true man', all of whose possibilities the initiate is called upon to realize in himself. This particular point deserves some further emphasis, however, for it could be objected that since manifestation in its entirety is and can only be the product of Heaven and Earth, every man and even every being whatsoever is equally and by that very fact a son of Heaven and Earth, since its nature necessarily participates in both; and in a sense this is true, for in every being there is indeed an essence and a substance in the relative sense of these terms, a *yang* aspect and a *yin* aspect, a side 'in act' and a side 'in potency', an 'interior' and an 'exterior'. But there are degrees to observe in this participation, for in manifested beings the celestial and terrestrial influences can obviously combine in many different ways and in

---

1. We even find traces of it in the ritual of an organization as completely deviated toward outward activity as Carbonarism; it is such vestiges, naturally misunderstood in a case like this, that bear witness to the truly initiatic origin of organizations that have thus reached such an extreme degree of deviation (see *Perspectives on Initiation*, chap. 12).

many different proportions, and it is this moreover that explains
their infinite diversity. That which each being is in a certain way and
to a certain degree, only Man—and by this we mean 'true man'[2]—is
fully and 'par excellence' in our state of existence, and it is he alone
who among his other privileges is given the capacity of recognizing
Heaven as his 'True Ancestor'.[3]

What we have just said is a direct and immediate consequence of
the properly 'central' position man occupies in relation to his own
state of existence,[4] or at least, to be more accurate, that he ought
normally and in principle to occupy, for this is how we should distinguish between ordinary man and 'true man'. 'True man', who
from the traditional point of view must alone be considered the
truly normal man, is so called because he truly possesses the fullness of human nature, for he has developed in himself the totality of
possibilities it implies; other men have only so to speak human
potentiality that is more or less developed in some aspects (generally this is the aspect that corresponds to the corporeal modality of
the individuality), but in any case it is far from being wholly 'actualized'; this predominantly potential character really makes them
sons of Earth far more than sons of Heaven, and it is also this that
makes them *yin* with regard to the Cosmos. For a man to be truly
'Son of Heaven and Earth', the 'act' in him must be equal to the
'potency', which implies the integral realization of his humanity,
that is to say the very condition of 'true man'. This is why 'true man'
is perfectly balanced between *yang* and *yin*, and also at the same
time why he is *yang* in relation to the Cosmos, for the celestial
nature is necessarily pre-eminent over the terrestrial wherever the
two are realized in equal measure; it is only thus that he can effectively fulfill the 'central' role that belongs to him as man, but on the
condition that he actually be man in the fullest sense of the word,

2. We shall not speak now of 'transcendent man', as we wish to reserve treatment of him for later; that is why it is only our particular state of existence that is in
question here, and not universal Existence in its integrality.

3. The expression 'True Ancestor' is among the designations of the *T'ien Ti
Huei*.

4. See *The Symbolism of the Cross*, chaps. 2 and 28.

and that in regard to all other manifested beings he be 'the image of the True Ancestor'.[5]

Now, it is important to remember that 'true man' is also 'primordial man', that is, his condition is that which was natural for humanity at its origins, and from which it has moved away bit by bit in the course of its terrestrial cycle to arrive where we now find what we have called the ordinary man, who is properly fallen man. This spiritual fall, which at the same time entails a disequilibrium with regard to *yang* and *yin*, can be described as a gradual separation from the center where 'primordial man' was situated; a being is less *yang* and more *yin* to the degree it is separated from the center, for in exactly the same measure the 'outward' predominates over the 'inward'; and this is why, as we said just now, he is then scarcely more than a 'son of Earth', less and less distinct 'in act' if not 'in potency' from the non-human beings that belong to the same level of existence. 'Primordial man', on the contrary, instead of being merely one of these beings, synthesized them all in his fully realized humanity;[6] by virtue of his 'interiority', embracing his entire state of existence just as Heaven embraces all manifestation (for it is in reality the center that contains all), he contained them as it were in himself as particular possibilities included in his own nature;[7] and that is why Man, as the third term of the Great Triad, effectively represents the totality of all manifested beings.

5. *Tao Te Ching*, chap. 4. This is the man who is 'created in the image of God', or more exactly in the image of *Elohim* or the celestial powers, and who moreover cannot really be such unless he is the 'Androgyne' constituted by the perfect equilibrium of *yang* and *yin*, according to the very words of Genesis (1:27): '*Elohim* created man in his own image [literally, 'his shadow', that is, his reflection], in the image of *Elohim* created He him; male and female created He them,' which is expressed in Islamic esoterism by the numerical equivalence of *Adam wa Hawā* and *Allah* (see *The Symbolism of the Cross*, chap. 3).

6. As we noted earlier, the Chinese term *Jen* can be translated as both 'Man' and 'Humanity', the latter being understood above all as human nature and not as the mere collectivity of men; in the case of 'true man', 'Man' and 'Humanity' are fully equivalent because he has integrally realized human nature in all its possibilities.

7. This is why, according to the symbolism of Genesis (2:19–20), Adam could truly 'name' all the beings of this world, that is, 'define' in the fullest sense of the word (implying determination and actualization at one and the same time) the

The 'place' where this 'true man' is situated is the central point where the powers of Heaven and Earth actually unite; he is by that very fact the direct and complete product of their union; and this is also why other beings, insofar as they are secondary and as it were partial productions, can only proceed from him according to an indefinite gradation determined by their greater or lesser separation from that same central point. It is because of this that, as we pointed out earlier, it is he alone who can properly be said in all truth to be the 'Son of Heaven and Earth'; he is so 'pre-eminently' and in the highest possible degree, while other beings are so only by participation, and he alone must be the means of this participation, for it is in his nature alone that Heaven and Earth are immediately united, if not in themselves, then at least by their respective influences in the domain of existence to which the human state belongs.[8]

As we have explained elsewhere,[9] initiation in its first part, which properly concerns the possibilities of the human state and constitutes what are called the 'lesser mysteries', has as its goal precisely the restoration of the 'primordial state'; in other words, through this initiation, if it is effectively realized, man is brought back from his present 'uncentered' condition to the central position which must normally be his, and is re-established in all the prerogatives inherent to that central situation.

'True man', then, is he who has effectively reached the end of the 'lesser mysteries', that is, the very perfection of the human state; because of this he is henceforth definitively established in the 'Invariable Middle' (*Chung Yung*), and thenceforth escapes the vicissitudes of the 'cosmic wheel', since the center does not participate in the movement of the wheel but is the fixed and immovable point

---

proper nature of each of them, which he knew immediately and inwardly as a dependency of his own nature. In this as in all things the Sovereign in the Far-Eastern tradition must play a role corresponding to that of 'primordial man': 'A wise prince gives to things the names that fit them, and each thing must be treated according to the meaning of the name he gives it' (*Lun Yu*, chap. 13).

8. This last restriction is required by the distinction that must be made between 'true man' and 'transcendent man', or between the perfected individual man as such and 'Universal Man'.

9. See in particular *Perspectives on Initiation*, chap. 39.

around which the movement occurs.[10] When he has arrived at this point, 'true man' has not yet attained the supreme degree, which is the final goal of initiation and the term of the 'greater mysteries'; but he has passed from circumference to center, from 'outward' to 'inward', and so truly fulfills the function of 'unmoved mover' with respect to the world that is his;[11] and the 'action of presence' belonging to this function imitates in its domain the 'non-acting' activity of Heaven.[12]

10. Cf. *The Symbolism of the Cross*, chap. 28, and *Perspectives on Initiation*, chap. 46.

11. One could say that he already no longer belongs to this world, but that it is on the contrary this world that belongs to him.

12. It is at least curious to see that in the West during the eighteenth century Martines de Pasqually claimed for himself the quality of 'true man'; regardless of whether his claim was justified or not, it can in any case be asked how he acquired knowledge of this specialized Taoist expression, which seems moreover to have been the only one he ever used.

10

MAN AND THE
THREE WORLDS

WHEN ONE COMPARES different traditional ternaries, even if it is possible to make them correspond term by term, one must be careful about concluding that the corresponding terms are necessarily identical, even when the terms are similarly designated, for it may well be that these terms are applied by analogical transposition to different levels. This observation is especially necessary when comparing the Far-Eastern Great Triad with the Hindu *Tribhuvana*. The 'three worlds' which make up the latter are Earth (*Bhū*), Air (*Bhuvas*), and Heaven (*Svar*); but this Heaven and Earth are not the *T'ien* and *Ti* of the Far-Eastern tradition, which always correspond to *Purusha* and *Prakriti* in the Hindu tradition.[1] Indeed, whereas these are outside of manifestation, of which they are the immediate principles, the 'three worlds' on the contrary represent the totality of manifestation itself divided into its three fundamental degrees, which are respectively the domain of supra-formal manifestation, the domain of subtle manifestation, and the domain of gross or corporeal manifestation.

This being so, in order to justify the use of words that one is obliged to translate by the same words 'Heaven' and 'Earth', it suffices to note that supra-formal manifestation is obviously that where celestial influences predominate, while gross manifestation is that where terrestrial influences predominate, using those expressions in the same sense we gave them earlier. We can also say, which amounts to the same thing, that the supra-formal realm is on the

---

1. See *Man and His Becoming according to the Vedānta*, chaps. 12 and 14.

side of essence while the gross realm is on the side of substance, without being able to identify them in any way with universal Essence and Substance themselves.[2] As for subtle manifestation, which forms the 'intermediary world' (*antariksha*), it is indeed a middle term in this regard and proceeds from the two categories of complementary influences in such proportion that it cannot be said that one clearly predominates over the other, at least as to the whole. Admittedly, in its very great complexity it contains some elements that are closer to the essential side of manifestation and some that are closer to the substantial side; but in any case all these elements are always on the side of substance with respect to supra-formal manifestation, and on the side of essence with respect to gross manifestation.

This middle term of the *Tribhuvana* must never be confused with that of the Great Triad, which is Man, although it does have a certain connection to it which is no less real for not being immediately apparent and which we shall point out shortly; but even so, it does not play the same role as the other from every point of view. Indeed, the middle term of the Great Triad is strictly the product or result of the two extremes, which is expressed by its traditional designation 'Son of Heaven and Earth'; here, on the contrary, subtle manifestation proceeds solely from supra-formal manifestation, and gross manifestation in its turn from subtle manifestation, that is, each term in descending order has its immediate principle in that which precedes it. It is thus not with respect to the order of the production of the terms that the concordance between these two ternaries can be validly established; there is only a 'static' correspondence as it

---

2. Let us mention incidentally in this connection that the characters 'paternal' and 'maternal' themselves that we spoke about in the last chapter are sometimes transposed in a similar way; for example, when 'Fathers above' and 'Mothers below' are spoken of, as they are in certain Arabic treatises, the 'Fathers' are the Heavens envisaged distinctively, that is, the supra-formal or spiritual states from which a being such as the human individual derives its essence, and the 'Mothers' are the elements from which the 'sublunary world' is constituted, that is, the corporeal world represented by the Earth insofar as it furnishes this same being its substance, and the terms 'essence' and 'substance' are naturally taken in a relative and particularized sense.

were when, once three terms have already been produced, the two extremes appear to correspond in a relative sense to essence and substance in the domain of universal manifestation taken in its entirety as being constituted analogously to a particular being, that is to say as the 'macrocosm' properly speaking.

There is no need to speak at length here of the constitutive analogy between 'macrocosm' and 'microcosm', about which we have already said enough in the course of other studies; but what must especially be remembered here is that a being such as man, as a 'microcosm', must necessarily participate in the 'three worlds' and have in himself elements that correspond to them respectively; and indeed, the same general ternary division is applicable to him as well: by his spirit he belongs to the domain of supra-formal manifestation, by his soul to that of subtle manifestation, and by his body to gross manifestation; we will return to this a bit later on and develop it further, for this will be an opportunity to show more precisely the relationships between some of the most important ternaries that can be considered. Moreover, it is man, and by this we must understand above all 'true man' or fully realized man, who, more than any other being is truly the 'microcosm', and this again by reason of his 'central' position, which makes him as it were an image, or rather a 'summary' (in the Latin sense of this word) of the entirety of manifestation, for his nature, as we explained earlier, synthesizes in itself that of all other beings, so that there can be nothing in manifestation that does not have in man its representation and correspondence. This is not merely a more or less 'metaphorical' way of speaking as the moderns are all too readily inclined to believe, but indeed the expression of a rigorous truth, on which a considerable part of the traditional sciences are based; here in particular lies the explanation of the correlations which exist, in the most 'positive' way, between modifications of the human order and those of the cosmic order, and which the Far-Eastern tradition emphasizes perhaps more than any other in order to draw from them all the practical applications they contain.

On the other hand, we have already alluded to a more particular correlation between man and the 'intermediary world', which is what could be called a correlation of 'function': situated between

Heaven and Earth, not only in the principial sense these words have in the Great Triad, but also in the more specialized sense they have in the *Tribhuvana*, that is to say between the spiritual world and the corporeal world, and participating in both at once by his makeup, man by this fact plays in regard to the entire Cosmos an intermediary role comparable to that played in the living being by the soul between spirit and body. Now what is particularly worthy of note in this regard is that it is precisely in this intermediary domain, which in its entirety is designated as 'soul' or again as 'subtle form', that we find the element properly characteristic of the human individuality as such, the 'mind' (*manas*), so that this specifically human element could be said to occupy the same place in man that man himself occupies in the Cosmos.

It should now be easy to understand that the function by which man corresponds to the middle term of the *Tribhuvana*, or to the soul which represents it in a living being, is properly a 'mediatory' function: the animating principle has often been described as the 'mediator' between the spirit and the body;[3] and in the same way man truly plays the role of 'mediator' between Heaven and Earth, as we will more fully explain later. It is in this respect only, and not insofar as man is 'Son of Heaven and Earth', that a term-by-term correspondence can be established between the Great Triad and the *Tribhuvana*, without this in any way implying an identification of the terms of the one ternary with those of the other; this is the point of view that we earlier called 'static' to distinguish it from that which could be called 'genetic',[4] that is, concerned with the order of the terms' production, for which such a concordance is no longer possible, as will be better seen in the considerations to follow.

3. One may remember here in particular Cudworth's 'plastic mediator'.

4. Although 'static' is usually opposed to 'dynamic', we prefer here not to use the word 'dynamic', which though not entirely improper does not express clearly enough what is involved.

11

SPIRITUS
ANIMA
CORPUS

THE TERNARY DIVISION is the most general and at the same time the simplest way that the composition of a living being can be defined, particularly that of man, for it is quite obvious that the Cartesian duality of 'spirit' and 'body' which has imposed itself on all modern Western thought can in no way correspond to reality; we have made this point often enough that there is no need to return to it now. The distinction of spirit, soul, and body is moreover that which has been unanimously accepted by all the traditional doctrines of the West, whether this be in antiquity or in the Middle Ages; that the West should later reach the point of forgetfulness where 'spirit' and 'soul' are seen only as kinds of rather vague synonyms, and where they can be used interchangeably even though they properly designate realities of totally different orders, is perhaps one of the most astonishing examples that could be given of the confusion characterizing the modern mentality. This error also has consequences that are not all purely theoretical, and for this reason it is obviously even more dangerous;[1] but it is not this that need occupy us now, and we wish only as regards the traditional ternary division to clarify certain points that have a direct bearing on the subject of our study.

This distinction between spirit, soul, and body has been applied to the 'macrocosm' as well as to the 'microcosm', for the composition

---

1. See *The Reign of Quantity and the Signs of the Times*, chap. 35.

of the one is analogous to that of the other, so that there are necessarily rigorously corresponding elements on both sides. Among the Greeks this way of thinking seems to be linked especially to the cosmological doctrine of the Pythagoreans, who really only 'adapted' teachings that were much more ancient. Plato was inspired by this doctrine and followed it far more closely than is ordinarily believed, and it was partly through him that something of this teaching was transmitted to later philosophers, for example the Stoics, whose much more exoteric point of view only too often mutilated and distorted the ideas in question. The Pythagoreans envisaged a fundamental quaternary comprising first of all the Principle, transcendent with respect to the Cosmos, then the universal Spirit and universal Soul, and finally the primordial *hyle*;[2] it is important to note that since this final term represents pure potentiality it cannot be assimilated to the body, and that it corresponds rather to the 'Earth' of the Great Triad than to that of the *Tribhuvana*, while the universal Spirit and universal Soul clearly correspond to the latter's other two terms. As for the transcendent Principle, it corresponds in certain respects to the 'Heaven' of the Great Triad, but on the other hand it is also identified with Being or metaphysical Unity, that is, *T'ai Chi*. There seems to be a lack of a clear distinction here, but perhaps this was not required by the point of view, much more cosmological than metaphysical, upon which the quaternary in question was established. However that may be, the Stoics distorted this teaching in a 'naturalistic' sense by losing sight of the transcendent Principle and envisaging no more than an immanent 'God' whom they identified simply with the *Spiritus Mundi;* we do not say with the *Anima Mundi* contrary to what some of their interpreters seem to believe, affected as they are by the modern confusion between spirit and soul, for in reality, both for them and for those who more faithfully followed traditional doctrine, the *Anima Mundi* has never had any but a purely 'demiurgic' role in the strictest sense of the word in the elaboration of the Cosmos from the primordial *hyle*.

---

2. The beginning of the *Rasā' il Ikhwan aṣ-Ṣafā'* [*The Brethren of Purity*] contains a very clear exposition of this Pythagorean doctrine.

We have just spoken of the elaboration of the Cosmos, but perhaps it would be more exact to speak of the formation of the *Corpus Mundi*, firstly because the 'demiurgic' function is properly a 'formative' one,[3] and next because in a certain sense the universal Spirit and universal Soul themselves form part of the Cosmos; we say 'in a certain sense', for in truth they can be considered from a double point of view, again corresponding in a way to what in our last chapter we referred to as the 'genetic' and the 'static' points of view, either as 'principles' (in a relative sense) or as constitutive 'elements' of the 'macrocosmic' being. This arises from the fact that, as soon as it is a question of manifested Existence, we are on this side of the distinction between Essence and Substance; from the 'essential' point of view, Spirit and Soul are, on different levels, like 'reflections' of the very Principle of manifestation; from the 'substantial' point of view they appear on the contrary as 'productions' drawn from *materia prima*, although they themselves determine its subsequent productions in a descending direction,[4] and this because if universal Spirit and universal Soul are to be effectively situated in manifestation, they must themselves become an integral part of universal manifestation. The connection between these two different points of view is represented symbolically by the complementarism of a luminous ray and its plane of reflection, which both are necessary to produce an image, so that on the one hand the image is truly a reflection of the luminous source itself, and on the other it is situated at the degree of reality marked by the plane of reflection;[5] to use the language of the Far-Eastern tradition, the luminous ray corresponds here to celestial influences, and the plane of reflection

3. It is important to note that we say 'formative', not 'creative'; this distinction will be more clear if it is recalled that the four terms of the Pythagorean quaternary can be correlated respectively with the 'four worlds' of the Hebrew Kabbalah.

4. Let us recall in this connection that according to Hindu doctrine *Buddhi*, which as pure Intellect corresponds to *Spiritus* and supra-formal manifestation, is itself the first of *Prakriti's* productions, but at the same time it is also the first degree of the manifestation of *Ātmā* or the transcendent Principle (see *Man and His Becoming according to the Vedānta*, chap. 7).

5. See *The Symbolism of the Cross,* chap. 24.

to terrestrial influences, which concurs with a consideration of the 'essential' and 'substantial' aspects of manifestation.[6]

Naturally, these remarks that we have just made in connection with the constitution of the 'macrocosm' apply just as well to the spirit and soul in the 'microcosm'; it is only the body that can never be considered properly speaking as a 'principle' because, as the result and final term of manifestation (this of course for our world or our state of existence) it is solely a 'product' and cannot become 'producer' in any respect. By this character the body, as completely as possible in the manifested order, expresses substantial passivity; but at the same time it thereby also distinguishes itself in the most obvious way from Substance itself, which as 'maternal' principle cooperates in the production of manifestation. In this regard, the ternary of spirit, soul, and body is, one might say, constituted differently from the ternaries formed of two complementary and as it were symmetrical terms and a product which occupies an intermediate position between them; in this case (and also—this goes without saying—in that of the *Tribhuvana* to which it corresponds exactly) the first two terms are both situated on the same side relative to the third term, and although in the final analysis this can still be considered as their product, they no longer play a symmetrical role in this production; the body has its immediate principle in the soul, but it proceeds from the spirit only indirectly and through the intermediary of the soul. It is only when we view the being as fully constituted thus from what we earlier called a 'static' point of view, that—considering the 'essential' aspect of the spirit and the 'substantial' aspect of the body—one can find in this respect a symmetry, no longer between the first two terms of the ternary, but between the first and the last; the soul is indeed then, in the same respect, the intermediary between spirit and body (and it is this that justifies its designation as 'mediating' principle, which we noted earlier), but it remains no less, as second term, necessarily anterior to

6. The luminous ray and the plane of reflection correspond exactly to the vertical and horizontal lines taken to symbolize Heaven and Earth respectively (see above, figure 7).

the third,[7] and consequently can never be regarded as a product or as a resultant of the two extreme terms.

Another question might be raised: how can it be that, despite the lack of symmetry we have just noted, the spirit and soul are nonetheless sometimes taken in a certain way as complementaries, spirit then generally being regarded as a masculine principle and soul as a feminine one? This is because the spirit is what is closest in manifestation to the essential pole, so that the soul is, relative to it, on the substantial side; thus in relation to each other spirit is *yang* and soul is *yin*, and this is why they are often symbolized respectively by the Sun and the Moon, which can moreover be justified even more fully by saying that the spirit is the light directly emanating from the Principle whereas the soul is only a reflection of this light. Moreover, the 'intermediary world', which can also be called the 'animic' domain, is properly the milieu where forms are elaborated, and this is in the final analysis a 'substantial' or 'maternal' role; and this elaboration is carried out through the action, or rather through the influence, of the spirit, which therefore plays in this respect an 'essential' or 'paternal' role; it must be understood, moreover, that for the spirit this can only be an 'action of presence' that imitates the 'non-acting' activity of Heaven.[8]

We will add a few words about the principal symbols of the *Anima Mundi*. One of the most common is the serpent by reason of the fact that the 'animic' world is the proper domain of cosmic forces, which although also acting in the corporeal world, belong in themselves to the subtle order; and this is naturally connected to

7. It goes without saying that the priority here is essentially logical, for the three terms are being considered simultaneously as constituent elements of the being.

8. These last remarks can help us understand why, in the Hermetic symbolism of the 28th degree of Scottish Freemasonry, *Spiritus* and *Anima* are represented respectively by the figures of the Holy Spirit and of the Virgin, which is a less universal application than that where they correspond to *Purusha* and *Prakriti*, as we said at the beginning. But it should be added that in this case, what is envisaged as the product of the two terms in question is not the body but something of another order, the Philosophers' Stone, often identified symbolically with Christ; and from this point of view their relationship conforms even more strictly to the notion of complementarism properly speaking than that concerning the production of corporeal manifestation.

what we said above about the symbolism of the double spiral and that of the caduceus; moreover, the duality of aspects with which the cosmic force is clothed corresponds very well with the intermediate character of this 'animic' world, which makes it prop-

erly the meeting place of both celestial and terrestrial influences.

On the other hand, as symbol of the *Anima Mundi*, the serpent is most commonly depicted in the circular form of the *Ouroboros*; in fact, this form is appropriate for the animic principle inasmuch as it is on the side of essence with respect to the corporeal world; but of course it is

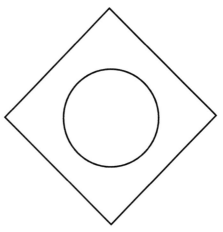

Figure 15

on the contrary on the side of substance with respect to the spiritual world, so that, depending on the point of view from which it is considered, it can take on the attributes of essence or of substance, which gives it so to speak the appearance of a double nature. These two aspects are united in a quite remarkable way in another symbol of the *Anima Mundi* belonging to medieval Hermeticism (figure 15): this is a circle within an 'animated' square, that is, a square standing on one of its corners to suggest the idea of movement, whereas a square resting on its base expresses on the contrary the idea of stability;[9] and what makes this figure particularly interesting from our present point of view is that the circular and square forms of which it is composed have here exactly the same meanings that they have in the Far-Eastern Tradition.[10]

---

9. See *The Reign of Quantity and the Signs of the Times*, chap. 20.

10. Comparing this figure with figure 8, one will note that the schematic representation of the 'intermediary world' seems to be as it were that of the entire Cosmos turned 'inside out'. It would be possible to deduce from this observation certain rather important consequences as regards subtle manifestation, but we cannot develop them here.

12

SULPHUR
MERCURY
SALT

CONSIDERATION OF THE TERNARY spirit, soul, and body leads us quite naturally to the alchemical ternary Sulphur, Mercury, and Salt,[1] for this is comparable to it in many respects although proceeding from a somewhat different point of view, something that appears particularly in the fact that here the complementarity of the first two terms is much more accentuated, whence a symmetry which, as we have seen, does not truly exist in the case of spirit and soul. What makes for one of the greatest difficulties in the understanding of alchemical or Hermetic writings in general is that the same terms are frequently taken according to multiple acceptations which correspond to different points of view; but if this is so in particularly with Sulphur and Mercury, it is no less true that the first is consistently viewed as an active or masculine principle and the second as a passive or feminine principle; as for Salt, it is so to speak neuter, as is altogether appropriate for the product of two complementaries in which the inverse tendencies inherent in their respective natures are balanced.

Without entering into details which would be out of place here, it can be said that Sulphur, whose active nature assimilates it to an

---

1. It should hardly be necessary to point out that there is no question here of the substances which bear these same names in ordinary chemistry, nor of anything corporeal whatsoever, but in reality of principles.

igneous principle, is essentially a principle of inner activity considered as radiating outward from the very center of the being. In man, or by analogy with him, this inner force is often identified in a certain way with the power of the will, but this is accurate only if we understand the will in a much deeper sense than its ordinary psychological meaning, in a manner analogous to the way it is used for example in 'Divine Will',[2] or in the Far-Eastern expression 'Will of Heaven'. The reason for this qualification is that the origin of will is properly 'central', while what psychology considers is merely 'peripheral' and relates in the final analysis only to superficial modifications of the being. Moreover, it is no accident that we have mentioned the 'Will of Heaven' here, for although it cannot be assimilated to Heaven itself, Sulphur by its 'inwardness' obviously belongs at least to the category of celestial influences; and as for its identification with the will, one can say that, if this is not truly applicable in the case of the ordinary man (whom psychology takes exclusively as its object of study), it is on the contrary justified in the case of 'true man', who is himself located at the center of all things and whose will in consequence is necessarily united with the 'Will of Heaven'.[3]

As for Mercury, its passivity correlative to the active nature of Sulphur has led to its being regarded as a principle of humidity;[4] and it is thought of as reacting from the outside, so that it plays in this regard the role of a centripetal and compressive force in opposition to the centrifugal and expansive action of Sulphur, which it also

2. Let us note in this connection that the Greek word *theion*, which is the term for sulphur, at the same time means 'divine'.

3. We shall come across this question later on in connection with the ternary 'Providence, Will, Destiny'. — 'Transcendent man', that is, he who has realized in himself 'Universal Man' (*al-insān al-kāmil*), is himself referred to in the language of Islamic Hermeticism as the 'red Sulphur' (*al-kabrīt al-aḥmar*), which is also represented symbolically by the Phoenix; between him and 'true man' or 'primordial man' (*al-insān al-qadīm*) the difference is the same as that between the work of 'reddening' and the work of 'whitening', which correspond to the respective perfections of the 'greater mysteries' and the 'lesser mysteries'.

4. This is why among its various designations is found the expression 'radical humidity'.

in a sense limits. By all these respectively complementary characteristics—activity and passivity, 'interiority' and 'exteriority',
expansion and contraction—it can be seen that, to return to Far-
Eastern terminology, Sulphur is *yang* and Mercury is *yin*, and that if
the first is related to the order of celestial influences, the second
must be related to that of terrestrial influences. However, one must
be very careful not to place Mercury in the corporeal domain but in
the subtle or 'animic' domain; by reason of its 'outward' character it
can be considered as representing the 'ambience', this being conceived as the totality of the currents of the dual cosmic force spoken
of earlier.[5] It is moreover by reason of the double nature or double
aspect of this force, which is an inherent characteristic of everything
belonging to the 'intermediary world', that Mercury, although primarily a principle of humidity as we just said, is nonetheless sometimes described as an 'igneous water' (and even alternately as a
'liquid fire'),[6] especially when it undergoes the action of Sulphur,
which 'elicits' this dual nature and causes it to pass from potency to
act.[7]

From the inward action of Sulphur and the outward reaction of
Mercury there results a kind of 'crystallization' that determines so to
speak a limit common to both inner and outer, or a neutral zone
where the opposing influences proceeding respectively from each

5. Recall what was said above about the double spiral regarded as a 'schema of
the ambience'; the Mercury of the Hermeticists is in the final analysis the same as
the 'astral light' of Paracelsus or what some more recent authors such as Eliphas
Lévi have more or less accurately called the 'great magical agent', although its use in
the domain of the traditional sciences is far from being limited to this lower application that constitutes magic in the strict sense of the word, as is sufficiently shown
moreover by our earlier considerations regarding Hermetic 'solution' and 'coagulation'. On the distinction between Hermeticism and magic, see also *Perspectives on
Initiation*, chap. 41.

6. The currents of subtle force can give this impression to those who perceive
them, and this may even be one of the causes of the illusion of 'fluidity' so often
associated with them, without prejudice to reasons of another order which may
also give rise to this illusion or help maintain it (cf. *The Reign of Quantity and the
Signs of the Times*, chap. 18).

7. It is then what the Hermeticists call 'animate' or 'double' Mercury in order to
distinguish it from ordinary Mercury, that is Mercury taken purely and simply for
what it is in itself.

meet and are stabilized; the product of this 'crystallization' is Salt,[8] which is represented by the cube insofar as the latter is at once the type of the crystalline form and the symbol of stability.[9] By the fact that it marks with respect to the individual manifestation of a being the separation of inward and outward, this third term constitutes for that being a kind of 'envelope' by which it is both in contact with the 'ambience' in a certain respect and isolated from it in another; in this it corresponds to the body, which plays this 'terminating' role in a case like that of the human individuality.[10] On the other hand, from the preceding we have seen the obvious relationship that Sulphur has with the spirit and that Mercury has with the soul; but here again it is necessary to pay the greatest attention when comparing two different ternaries to the fact that the correspondence of

8. There is an analogy with the formation of a salt in the chemical sense of the word in that this is produced by the combination of an acid, the active element, with an alkali, the passive element, which in this case play roles comparable respectively to those of Sulphur and Mercury, but which of course differ essentially from them in that they are bodies and not principles; salt is neutral and generally occurs in a crystalline form, which succeeds in justifying the Hermetic transposition of that designation.

9. This is the 'cubic stone' of Masonic symbolism; but it is necessary to specify that this is the ordinary 'cubic stone' and not the 'pointed cubic stone' which properly symbolizes the philosophers' stone, for the pyramid surmounting the cube represents a spiritual principle that establishes itself on the base constituted by the Salt. It can be noted that the planar outline of this 'pointed cubic stone' is a square surmounted by a triangle, which differs from the alchemical sign for Sulphur only by the substitution of the square for the cross. The two symbols have the same numerical correspondence, $7 = 3 + 4$, where the septenary is composed of an upper ternary and a lower quaternary which are relatively 'celestial' and 'terrestrial' with respect to each another; but the alteration of the cross into a square expresses the 'fixation' or 'stabilization' as a permanent 'entity' of what ordinary Sulphur manifested only in a state of 'virtuality' and which it would not have been able to realize except by taking a point of support in the very resistance offered to it by Mercury as 'matter of the work'.

10. From what was said in the preceding note the reader will be able to understand the importance of the body (or of a 'terminating' element corresponding to it in the conditions of another state of existence) as a 'support' for initiatic realization. Let us add here that if Mercury is the 'matter of the work' as we have just said, Salt becomes so subsequently and in another respect, as the formation of the symbol of the 'pointed cubic stone' shows. It is to this that the distinction made by the Hermeticists between their 'first matter' and their 'subsequent matter' refers.

their terms can vary according to the viewpoint from which they are envisaged. Indeed, as 'animic principle', Mercury actually corresponds to the 'intermediary world' or to the median term of the *Tribhuvana*, and Salt, insofar as it is, we will not say identical, but at least comparable to the body, occupies the same terminal position as the domain of gross manifestation; but in another connection the respective situations of these two terms appear as the inverse of this, that is to say that Salt then becomes the median term. It is this latter point of view which is most characteristic of the specifically Hermetic conception of the ternary in question because of the symmetrical role it assigns to Sulphur and Mercury: Salt is then intermediate between them, first because it is like their resultant, and next because it is situated at the very limit of the 'inner' and 'outer' domains to which they respectively correspond; it is 'terminal' in this sense, one could say, even more than in relation to the process of manifestation, although in reality the one does not exclude the other.

This should enable us to understand why Salt cannot be equated with the body without further reservation; one can only say that the body corresponds to Salt in a certain respect or in a particular application of the alchemical ternary. In another, less restricted application, it is the entire individuality that corresponds to Salt;[11] in this case Sulphur is always the inward principle of the being and Mercury is the subtle 'ambience' of a given world or state of existence; the individuality (assuming of course that it is a case of formal manifestation, such as the human state) is the resultant of the meeting of the inward principle with the 'ambience'; and one can say that the being insofar as it is manifested in this state is as it were 'enveloped'

---

11. From this point of view the transformation of the 'rough-hewn stone' into the 'cubic stone' represents the development which the ordinary individuality must undergo to become capable of serving as a 'support' or 'base' for initiatic realization; the 'pointed cubic stone' represents the effective adjunction to that individuality of a principle of a supra-individual order constituting the initiatic realization itself, which can moreover be envisaged in an analogous way and hence represented by the same symbol in its different degrees, these degrees always being obtained by operations that correspond to each other, although at different levels, as in the 'whitening' and' reddening' of the alchemists.

in the individuality, in a way analogous to that in which, at another level, the individuality itself is 'enveloped' in the body. Turning again to a symbolism used earlier, Sulphur is comparable to the luminous ray and Mercury to its plane of reflection, and Salt is the product of the meeting of the first with the second; but this, which raises the whole question of the relationship of a being to the environment in which it manifests itself, deserves to be more amply treated.

13

THE BEING AND
ITS ENVIRONMENT

IN THE INDIVIDUAL NATURE of every being there are two elements
of different orders that must be carefully distinguished, while at
the same time indicating their relationship as precisely as possible.
This individual nature proceeds first from what the being is in itself
and represents its inward and active side, and then, secondarily,
from the totality of the influences of the environment in which it
manifests itself, which represents its outward and passive side. To
understand how the constitution of the individuality (and it must
of course be understood that it is a question here of the integral
individuality, the corporeal modality of which is only its most outward aspect) is determined by the action of the first of these two
elements on the second, or in alchemical terms, how Salt results
from the action of Sulphur on Mercury, we can use the geometrical
representation just alluded to in speaking of the luminous ray and
its plane of reflection;[1] and for this we must relate the first element
to the vertical dimension and the second to the horizontal. The
vertical will then represent that which connects all the different
states of manifestation of one and the same being, and which is necessarily the expression of that same being, or if one wishes, its 'personality', the direct projection by which it is reflected in all states,
while the horizontal plane will represent the domain of a certain
state of manifestation, envisaged here in the 'macrocosmic' sense;

---

1. For a detailed study of this geometrical representation, we return as always to
our study *The Symbolism of the Cross*.

consequently, the manifestation of the being in this state will be determined by the intersection of the vertical axis in question with this horizontal plane.

This being so, it is obvious that this point of intersection is not just anywhere, but is itself determined by the vertical in question, inasmuch as it is distinguished from every other vertical, that is, in the final analysis, by the fact that this being is what it is and not some other being also manifesting itself in the same state. One could say in other words that it is the individual being itself which, by its own nature, determines the conditions of its manifestation, with the reservation of course that these conditions cannot in any case be anything except a specification of the general conditions of the state in question, since its manifestation must necessarily be a development of possibilities contained in that state to the exclusion of those which belong to other states; and this qualification is represented geometrically by the previous determination of the horizontal plane.

The being, then, will manifest itself by clothing itself, so to speak, in elements borrowed from the environment, and the 'crystallization' of these elements will be determined by the action on the environment of its own internal nature (which in itself must be considered to be of an essentially supra-individual order, as indicated by the vertical direction in which it exercises its action); in the case of the individual human state, these elements will naturally belong to the different modalities of that state, that is, both to the corporeal order and to the subtle or psychic order. This point is particularly important to grasp if one is to avoid certain difficulties due to erroneous or incomplete conceptions; indeed, if we translate this more particularly in terms of 'heredity', we can say that there is not only a physiological heredity but also a psychic heredity, both explained in exactly the same way, that is, by the presence in the individual's constitution of elements derived from the particular environment in which his birth took place. But in the West some people refuse to admit a psychic heredity because they do not know anything beyond the domain to which it belongs and believe that it is this domain that properly belongs to the being itself, which represents what it is completely independent of all influence from the environment. There are others who on the contrary grant the existence of this heredity but believe they can conclude from this that everything that belongs to the being is entirely determined by the environment, that it is nothing more nor less than what this makes it to be, because they too do not conceive of anything outside of the corporeal and psychic domains. There are thus two errors here that are in a way opposed, but which have a single source; both reduce the entire being to its individual manifestation, and they both likewise ignore any principle transcendent to it. At the root of all these modern conceptions of the human being is always the Cartesian dualism of 'body' and 'soul',[2] which in fact is purely and simply the duality of the physiological and the psychic, considered improperly as being irreducible, ultimate in a way, and as embracing the whole being within its two terms, whereas in reality these latter terms represent only the superficial and exterior aspects of the manifested being and are no more than simple modalities belonging to one and the same degree of existence, the degree represented by the horizontal plane we have been considering, so that the one is no less contingent than the other, and the true being is beyond them both.

Returning now to heredity, we must add that it does not integrally explain the influences exerted on an individual by the environment but is only its most readily perceptible part; in reality, these influences extend much further, and one could even say without exaggeration and in the most literally exact way that they extend indefinitely in all directions. In fact, the cosmic environment, which is the domain of the state of manifestation under consideration, can be conceived only as a whole all of whose parts are linked to each other without any break in continuity, for to conceive it otherwise would amount to assuming in it the existence of a 'void', whereas this is not a possibility of manifestation and can have no place there.[3] In consequence, there must necessarily be relationships, that is to say, in the final analysis, reciprocal actions and reactions,

---

2. We deliberately use the terms 'body' and 'soul' rather than 'body' and 'spirit' because in fact it is always the soul that in such cases is abusively taken for the spirit, which in reality is wholly unknown.

3. See *The Multiple States of the Being*, chap. 3.

between all the individual beings manifested in this domain, either simultaneously or successively;[4] from the closest to the furthest (understood temporally as well as spatially), this is essentially only a question of differing proportions or degrees, so that heredity, whatever its relative importance with respect to all the rest, no longer appears as anything more than a particular case.

In every case, whether we are dealing with hereditary influences or others, what we said at the beginning always remains equally true: a being's situation in the environment is in the last analysis determined by its own nature, and the elements which it takes from its immediate ambience, as well as those it attracts as it were to itself from the indefinite totality of its domain of manifestation (and this of course applies to elements of the subtle order as well as to that of the corporeal order), must necessarily correspond with that nature, without which it could not effectively assimilate them in such a way as to make them so many secondary modifications of itself. It is in this that lies the 'affinity' by which the being, so to speak, takes from its environment only what conforms to the possibilities it bears within itself, those which belong to it alone and to no other being, and which, in virtue of this very conformity, must furnish the contingent conditions that permit these possibilities to develop or be 'actualized' in the course of its individual manifestation.[5] Moreover, it is obvious that for any relationship between any two beings to be real it must necessarily be the expression of something belonging to the natures of both; thus the influence that a being appears to undergo from the outside and to receive from another being is, when considered from a deeper point of view, nothing but a sort of

---

4. This relates to the point of view corresponding to the horizontal direction in the geometrical representation; if one considers things according to the vertical direction, this solidarity between all beings is seen to be a consequence of the principial Unity itself from which all existence necessarily proceeds.

5. These conditions are what are sometimes called 'occasional causes', but it goes without saying that they are not causes in the true sense of the word, although they may appear to be so when looked at from the most outward point of view. The true causes of everything that happens to a being are in the final analysis always the possibilities inherent in the very nature of that being, that is, something of a purely interior order.

translation with respect to the environment of a possibility inherent in the proper nature of the being itself.[6]

There is a sense, however, in which it can be said that a being is truly subject in its manifestation to the influence of the environment; but this is only inasmuch as that influence is considered with regard to its negative side, that is, inasmuch as it is for that particular being a limitation. This is an immediate consequence of the conditioned character of every state of manifestation; the being is subject to certain conditions that have a limitative role and that include, first, the general conditions defining the state in question, and then the special conditions defining that being's particular mode of manifestation in that state. Besides, it is easy to understand that whatever the appearances limitation as such has no positive existence, that it is nothing more than a restriction excluding certain possibilities or a 'privation' with respect to what it thus excludes, that is, however we may choose to express it, something purely negative.

On the other hand, it must be carefully understood that such limiting conditions essentially inhere in one particular state of manifestation, that they apply exclusively to whatever is included in that state, and that consequently they could never belong to the being itself and follow it into another state. Naturally, in order to manifest itself in this other state, the being will also meet with certain conditions that are analogous to but different from those to which it was subject in the state we first considered and which cannot be described in terms appropriate solely to these; just as human language, for example, cannot express conditions of existence other than those of the corresponding state, since this language is in the final analysis determined and as it were fashioned by those very conditions. We dwell on this because, although it is easy to admit without great difficulty that the elements taken from the environment enter into the constitution of the human individuality, something that is properly a 'fixation' or 'coagulation' of those elements must

6. Cf. what we said elsewhere in connection with the qualifications for initiation on the subject of infirmities of an apparently accidental origin (*Perspectives on Initiation*, chap. 14).

be given to it by 'solution' once this individuality has ended its cycle of existence and the being has passed to another state, as everyone can observe directly, at least for elements of the corporeal order;[7] it seems less easy to admit that, although the two things are really closely related, the being departs entirely from the conditions to which it was subject in this individual state;[8] and this fact doubtless stems above all from the impossibility, certainly not of conceiving but of imagining, conditions of existence altogether different from the former, and for which no term of comparison can be found in that state.

An important implication of what we have just noted is related to the fact that an individual being belongs to a certain species, such as the human species for example; there is obviously something in the very nature of that being that determined its birth into this species rather than into any other;[9] but on the other hand, it will thereupon be subject to the conditions implied in the very definition of the species and which will be among the special conditions of its mode of existence as an individual; these are, one could say, the two aspects, 'positive' and 'negative', of the specific nature: positive as the domain of manifestation of certain possibilities, negative as a limited condition of existence. However, what must be carefully understood is that it is only as a manifested individual in the state under consideration that the being effectively belongs to the species in question, and that, in every other state, it escapes it entirely and is no longer linked to it in any way whatsoever. In other words, consideration of the species applies only in the 'horizontal' sense, that is, in the domain of a particular state of existence; it can in no way intervene in a vertical sense, that is, when the being passes to other states. Of course, what is true in this respect for the species is also

---

7. We should add that bodily death does not necessarily coincide with a change of state in the strict sense of the word, and that it may only represent a simple change of modality within one and the same state of individual existence; but keeping all proportions, the same considerations apply in both cases.

8. Or only a part of the conditions where it is just a case of a change of modality, such as the passage from human individuality to an extra-corporeal modality.

9. It is significant in this respect that the Sanskrit word *jāti* means both 'birth' and 'species' or 'specific nature'.

true, and all the more so, for race, for family, in a word for all the more or less restricted portions of the individual domain in which by the conditions of its birth, the being is included by its manifestation in the state in question.[10]

By way of bringing these considerations to a close, we will add a few words about how, on the basis of what has just been said, what are called 'astral influences' can be envisaged. In the first place it should be made clear that this expression is not to be understood exclusively, or even principally, in terms of the influences of the stars themselves, by whose name [*astres*] they are designated, although these influences, like those of any other things, doubtless have their reality in their own order, but that these stars above all represent symbolically (which does not at all mean 'ideally' or in a more or less figurative way, but on the contrary by virtue of the effective and precise correspondences founded on the very makeup of the 'macrocosm') the synthesis of all the different categories of cosmic influences that have an effect on the individuality, the greater part of which belong to the subtle order. To regard the 'astral influences', as is usually done, as dominating the individuality, is to take only the most outward point of view; in a more profound order the truth is that, if the individuality is connected with a definite group of influences, it is because this group of influences is that very one that is in conformity with the nature of the being manifesting itself in that individuality. Thus, if 'astral influences' seem to determine what the individual is, this is nevertheless only an appearance; at root, they do not determine it but only express it by reason of the accord or harmony that necessarily exists between the individual and its environment, without which the individual could

---

10. Naturally, the case of caste is no exception here; this results, more visibly than for any other case, from the definition of caste as the very expression of the individual nature (*varṇa*), and so to speak as one with it, which indicates clearly that it does not exist except insofar as the being is considered within the limitations of the individuality, and that, if it necessarily exists insofar as it is contained within these limits, it cannot subsist beyond these limits, for all that constitutes its raison d'être is found exclusively within them and cannot be transposed into another domain of existence where the individual nature in question no longer corresponds to any possibility.

never realize the possibilities whose development constitutes the very course of its existence. The true determination does not come from the outside but from the being itself (which amounts to saying that in the formation of Salt it is Sulphur which is the active principle, whereas Mercury is only the passive principle), and the outward signs simply make it possible to discern it by giving it as it were a sensible expression, at least for those who can interpret them correctly.[11] This does nothing to change the results that can be drawn from an investigation of 'astral influences'; but from a doctrinal point of view it seems to us essential in order to understand their true role, that is, in the final analysis, the true nature of the relationships of the being with the environment in which its individual manifestation takes place, for what is expressed through these influences in an intelligibly coordinated form is the indefinite multitude of different elements which constitute this entire environment. There is no need to dwell further on this, for we think we have already said enough to convey how every individual participates to some degree in a double nature, which can in alchemical terms be called 'sulphurous' with regard to the inward and 'mercurial' as to the outward; and it is this double nature, fully realized and perfectly balanced in the 'true man', that effectively makes him the 'Son of Heaven and Earth', and that at the same time qualifies him to fulfill the function of 'mediator' between these two poles of manifestation.

11. It is this, moreover, that in a general way is the very principle of all the 'divinatory' applications of traditional sciences.

14

THE MEDIATOR

HE ascends from Earth to Heaven and descends again from Heaven to Earth; thereby he acquires the virtue and efficacity of things above and things below.

These words of the Hermetic Emerald Tablet can be applied very precisely to Man as the median term of the Great Triad, that is to say insofar as he is the 'mediator' by which communication is effectively established between Heaven and Earth.[1] This 'ascent from Earth to Heaven' is moreover represented ritually in very different traditions by climbing a tree or pole symbolizing the 'World Axis'; by this ascent, which is necessarily followed by a re-descent (and this double movement again corresponds to the stages of 'solution' and 'coagulation'), he who truly realizes what is implied in the rite thereby assimilates the celestial influences and brings them back as it were into this world to unite them with the terrestrial influences, first in himself, and later, by participation and by a kind of 'radiation', in the entire Cosmic environment.[2]

---

1. The same words can also be seen from the properly initiatic point of view as a very clear delineation of the twofold 'ascending' and 'descending' realization; but this is another point which we cannot develop at present. [See *Initiation and Spiritual Realization*, chap. 32. ED.]

2. In this connection we will note in passing that since the descent of celestial influences is often symbolized by rain, it is easy to understand the deeper meaning of those rites apparently aimed at rain-making; this meaning is obviously entirely independent of the 'magical' application which is commonly the only one seen in it, and which, while it cannot be denied, should be reduced to its true value as a contingency of a very inferior order.

It is interesting to observe that the symbolism of rain has even been preserved, by way of the Hebrew tradition, in the Catholic liturgy itself: *Rorate Coeli desuper, et*

The Far-Eastern tradition, along with many others,[3] states that in the beginning Heaven and Earth were not separated; and indeed, they were necessarily united and 'undifferentiated' in *T'ai Chi*, their common principle; but in order for manifestation to be produced it was necessary that Being be polarized into Essence and Substance, which can be described as a 'separation' of the two complementary terms which are represented as Heaven and Earth, since it is between them, or in the 'gap' between them if one may use such an expression, that the manifestation itself must be situated.[4] Thenceforward their communication can only be established along the axis that links together the centers of all the indefinitely manifold states of existence whose hierarchy constitutes universal manifestation, and which thus extends from one pole to the other, that is, precisely, from Heaven to Earth, as it were measuring the distance between them, as we said earlier, along the vertical dimension that marks the hierarchy of the states.[5] The center of each state can then be considered as the trace of this vertical axis on the horizontal plane which geometrically represents that state; and this center, which is properly the 'Invariable Middle' (*Chung Yung*), is by this very fact for that particular state the unique point where the union of celestial and terrestrial influences is effected, while at the same time it is also the only one from which a direct communication with the other states

nubes pluant Justum [Shower, O heaven, from above, and let the skies rain down righteousness] (Isaiah 45:8). The 'righteousness' in question can be regarded as the 'mediator' who 'descends again from Heaven to Earth,' or as the being that, effectively in full and conscious possession of its celestial nature, appears in this world as the *Avatāra*.

3. Of course, as to its basis, this agreement extends to all traditions without exception; but we mean to say that the very manner of expression in question is not exclusive to the Far-Eastern tradition.

4. Moreover, this can be applied analogically at different levels, according to whether what is being considered is universal manifestation in its entirety, or only a particular state of manifestation, that is to say a world, or even a more or less limited cycle in the existence of that world. In every case there will always be in the beginning something that corresponds in a more or less relative sense to the 'separation of Heaven and Earth'.

5. On the significance of this vertical axis, cf. *The Symbolism of the Cross*, chap. 23.

of existence is possible, this communication having necessarily to take place along the axis itself. Now as far as our own state is concerned, the center is man's normal 'place', which amounts to saying that 'true man' is identical with the center itself; it is thus in him and by him alone that, for this state, the union of Heaven and Earth is accomplished, and this is why all that is manifested within this same state proceeds from and depends entirely on him and exists only as it were as an outward and partial projection of his own possibilities. It is he also who, by his 'action of presence', maintains and preserves the existence of this world,[6] for he is the center and without a center nothing can effectively exist. This is the fundamental reason for the rites in every tradition that affirm in sensible form man's intervention for the maintenance of the cosmic order, and which in the final analysis are only so many more or less particular expressions of the function of 'mediator' which belongs to him essentially.[7]

There are many traditional symbols which represent Man, the middle term of the Great Triad, as placed between Heaven and Earth and thus fulfilling his role of 'mediator'; first we shall note in this connection that this is the general meaning of the trigrams of the *I Ching*, whose three lines correspond respectively to the three terms of the Great Triad; the top line symbolizes Heaven, the central line Man, and the bottom line Earth; we shall have to return to this below. In the hexagrams, the two superposed trigrams also correspond in their entirely to Heaven and to Earth respectively; here the middle term is no longer visibly depicted; but it is the hexagram itself as a whole that, by uniting the celestial influences with the terrestrial influences, properly expresses the function of 'mediator'. In this connection, a comparison is necessary with one of the meanings of the 'Seal of Solomon', which is also formed of six lines

6. In Islamic esoterism such a being is said to 'uphold the world by his breathing alone.'

7. We say 'expressions' insofar as these rites symbolically represent the function in question; but it must be understood that at the same time it is by the accomplishment of these same rites that man effectively and consciously fulfills that function; this is an immediate consequence of the efficacity inherent in rites, and which we have explained sufficiently elsewhere not to need to stress it again here (see *Perspectives on Initiation*).

although arranged in a different way; in this case, the upright triangle represents celestial nature and the inverted triangle represents
terrestrial nature, and the whole symbolizes 'Universal Man' who,
uniting these two natures in himself, is thereby the 'mediator' par
excellence.[8]

Another rather well-known Far-Eastern symbol is the tortoise,
placed between the upper and lower parts of its shell like Man
between Heaven and Earth; and in this representation the very form
of these two parts is no less significant than their placement: the
upper part, which 'covers' the animal, corresponds again to Heaven
by its rounded form, and likewise, the lower part, which 'supports'
it, corresponds to Earth by its flatness.[9] The whole shell is therefore
an image of the Universe,[10] and between its two parts the tortoise
itself naturally represents the middle term of the Great Triad, that is
to say Man; in addition, its withdrawal into the interior of its shell
symbolizes concentration in the 'primordial state', which is the state
of 'true man'; and this concentration is moreover the realization of
the plenitude of human possibilities, for although the center is
apparently only a point without extension, it is nonetheless this
point which, principially, really contains all things,[11] and this is precisely why 'true man' contains in himself everything that is manifested in the state of existence with whose center he is identified.

It is to a symbolism similar to that of the tortoise that, as we
noted in passing earlier,[12] the clothing worn by the ancient princes

8. In specifically Christian terms, this is the union of the divine and human
natures in Christ, who indeed has the character of 'mediator' par excellence (cf. *The
Symbolism of the Cross*, chap. 28). — The idea of 'Universal Man' extends to manifestation as a whole, by analogical transposition, the role which 'true man' exercises
in fact with respect to a particular state of existence.

9. A plane surface is naturally related directly to the straight line, an element of
the square, and both can equally be defined in a negative way by the absence of any
curvature.

10. This is why it is said that the diagram called *Lo Chu* was presented to Yü the
Great by a tortoise; and from this also derives the use made of the tortoise in certain
special applications of the traditional sciences, notably in the 'divinatory' order.

11. On the relation between point and extension see *The Symbolism of the Cross*,
chaps. 16 and 29.

12. The *Reign of Quantity and the Signs of the Times*, chap. 20.

of China had to have a round shape at the top (that is, at the neck) and a square form at the bottom, it being these forms that represent Heaven and Earth respectively; and we may note at this point that this symbol is very closely related to that which places Man between the square and the compasses, which we shall return to below, for these are the instruments which serve to draw the square and the circle respectively. In this arrangement of clothing it can also be seen that, as effectively uniting Heaven and Earth, the archetypal man represented by the prince appeared to be touching Heaven with his head while his feet rested on Earth; this is something that we shall meet again shortly in still greater detail. Let us add that if the clothing of the prince or sovereign thus had a symbolic meaning, it was the same for all the actions of his life, which were exactly regulated according to rites that, as we just said, made him the representation of the archetypal man in all circumstances; moreover, in the beginning he had truly to be a 'true man'; and if he could not always remain so later because of the growing spiritual degeneration of humanity, he still invariably continued to 'incarnate' 'true man' as it were, and to ritually take his place in the exercise of his function and independently of what he may have been in himself, and this all the more necessarily in that, as will be seen even more clearly later, his function was essentially that of 'mediator'.[13]

A characteristic example of these ritual actions is the Emperor's circumambulation of the Ming T'ang. Since we will treat this subject more fully later, we will content ourselves for the moment with saying that the Ming T'ang was like an image of the Universe,[14] concentrated as it were in a place that represented the 'Invariable Middle' (and the very fact that the Emperor resided in that place made him the representation of the 'true man'); and this was so under the double aspect of space and time, for in it the spatial symbolism of the cardinal points was directly related to the temporal symbolism of the seasons and the course of the annual cycle. Now the roof of that

13. We have already emphasized on other occasions the distinction that must be made in a general way between a traditional function and the individual fulfilling that function, what properly belongs to the first being independent of the worth of the second in himself (see especially Perspectives on Initiation, chap. 45).

14. Like the tortoise to whose symbolism it was attached, as we shall see, by the diagram of Lo Chu that furnished its plan.

edifice had a round shape, while its base was a square or rectangle; between this roof and base, which recalled the upper and lower parts of the tortoise's shell, the Emperor thus represented Man between Heaven and Earth. Moreover, this arrangement constitutes an architectural type that is found very generally and with the same symbolic value in a great number of different traditional forms; one can see this in examples such as the Buddhist *stūpas* and the Islamic *qubbah*, and many others, as we shall perhaps have the occasion to show more completely in another study, for this subject is among those which have a great importance concerning the properly initiatic meaning of the symbolism of building.

We will cite yet another symbol that is equivalent to this with respect to what we are presently considering; this is the chieftain in his chariot; the chariot was in fact constructed on the same 'cosmic models' as traditional buildings such as the *Ming T'ang*, with a circular canopy representing Heaven and square floor representing Earth. And we should add that both canopy and floor were connected by a pole, an axial symbol,[15] of which a small section even projected above the canopy[16] as if to show that the 'pinnacle of Heaven' is in reality beyond Heaven itself; and this pole was regarded as measuring symbolically the height of the prototypal man to whom the chieftain was likened, a height given by numerical proportions which varied moreover according to the cyclical conditions of the epoch. In this way, man himself was identified with the 'World Axis' in order to effectively link Heaven and Earth. We should add moreover that this identification with the axis, if regarded as fully effective, belongs more properly to 'transcendent man', whereas 'true man' is only identified effectively with one point on the axis, which is the center of his state, and thereby virtually with the axis itself. But this question of the relationship between 'true man' and 'transcendent man' demands yet other developments that will find their place in the later part of this study.

15. This axis is not always represented visibly in the traditional buildings we have just mentioned, but whether it is or not, it always plays a principal role in their construction, which is set out entirely with reference to it.

16. This detail, which is found in other cases, notably in the *stupa*, has a far greater importance than appears at first sight, for from the initiatic point of view it relates to the symbolic representation of the 'exit from the Cosmos'.

15

BETWEEN THE SQUARE
AND THE COMPASSES

ONE POINT WHICH OCCASIONS a most remarkable comparison
between the Far-Eastern tradition and the initiatic traditions of the
West is the symbolism of the compasses and the square. As we have
already pointed out, these manifestly correspond to the circle and
the square,[1] that is, to the geometrical figures representing respectively Heaven and Earth.[2] In Masonic symbolism, in conformity
with this correspondence, the compasses are normally placed above
and the square below;[3] between the two is generally represented a
figure of the Blazing Star, which is a symbol of Man,[4] and more precisely of 'regenerate man',[5] which thus completes the representation
of the Great Triad. Moreover, it is said that 'a Master Mason is
always found between the square and the compasses', in other words

---

1. We will note that in English the same word *square* denotes both the tool and
the figure; in Chinese, *fang* has the same two meanings.
2. The different ways of positioning the compasses and the square in relation to
each other in the three degrees of Craft Masonry show the celestial influences first
dominated by the terrestrial influences, then gradually freeing themselves from
them, and finally dominating them in their turn.
3. When these positions are reversed the symbol takes on a particular meaning
that is to be compared with the inversion of the alchemical symbol of Sulphur as
representing the accomplishment of the 'Great Work', just as with the symbolism of
the twelfth arcana of the Tarot.
4. The Blazing Star is a star of 5 points, and 5 is the number of the 'microcosm';
this correlation is moreover expressly indicated in cases where the star contains the
actual figure of a man (the head, the arms, and the legs being identified with its 5
points), as seen in Agrippa's pentagram.
5. According to an ancient ritual 'the Blazing Star is the symbol of the Mason
[one could say more generally, of the initiate] shining with light in the midst of the

in the very 'place' in which the Blazing Star is inscribed, and which is properly the 'Invariable Middle'.[6] The Master is therefore likened to 'true man', placed between Heaven and Earth and exercising the function of 'mediator'; and this is all the more exact in that, symbolically and 'virtually' at least if not effectively, Mastership represents the achievement of the 'lesser mysteries', of which the state of 'true man' is precisely the term;[7] it will be seen that here we have a symbolism that is rigorously equivalent to that we previously encountered in several different forms in the Far-Eastern tradition.

In connection with what we have just said about the character of Mastership, let us also point out in passing that this character, which belongs to the final grade in Freemasonry properly speaking, is well in agreement with the fact that, as we have noted elsewhere,[8] the craft initiations and those derived from them all relate to the 'lesser mysteries'. It should be added that in what are called the 'higher grades', formed from elements of rather diverse provenance, there are references to the 'greater mysteries', of which at least one is directly related to ancient Operative Masonry, which shows that this opened at least certain perspectives on what lies beyond the term of the 'lesser mysteries': we mean the distinction made in Anglo-Saxon Masonry between Square Masonry and Arch Masonry. In fact, in the transition 'from square to arch', or, to use the equivalent expressions from eighteenth-century French Freemasonry 'from triangle

darkness [of the profane world].' This is an obvious allusion to the words of the Gospel of Saint John [1:5]: *Et lux in tenebris lucet, et tenebrae eam non comprehenderunt.*

6. It is therefore not without reason that the Lodge of the Masters is also called the 'Middle Chamber'.

7. In connection with the Masonic formula just cited, it can be noted that the Chinese expression 'under Heaven' (*T'ien hsia*) which we have already mentioned and which designates the cosmos as a whole is susceptible of assuming, from the properly initiatic point of view, a particular meaning corresponding to the 'Temple of the Holy Spirit, which is everywhere' and which is the meeting place of the Brothers of the Rose-Cross, who are also 'true men' (see *Perspectives on Initiation*, chaps. 37 and 38). — We will also recall in this connection that 'Heaven covers' and that Masonic activities must be carried out, precisely, 'under cover', the Lodge itself moreover being an image of the Cosmos (see *The King of the World*, chap. 7).

8. *Perspectives on Initiation*, chap. 39.

to circle',[9] we find the opposition between square (or more generally, rectilinear) figures and circular figures, insofar as they correspond respectively to Earth and to Heaven. This can only therefore be a passage from the human state, represented by Earth, to the supra-human states, represented by Heaven (or the Heavens),[10] that is, a passage from the domain of the 'lesser mysteries' to that of the 'greater mysteries'.[11]

Returning to the parallel that we referred to at the outset, we must add that in Far-Eastern tradition the compasses and square are not only supposed implicitly as serving to trace the circle and the square, but that they also appear there explicitly in certain cases, particularly as attributes of Fu Hsi and Niu Kua, as we have already pointed out on another occasion;[12] but we did not offer any explanation there of a feature which at first sight might seem to be an anomaly in this regard and which remains to be explained. In effect, the 'compasses', as a 'celestial' symbol and therefore *yang* or masculine, properly belongs to Fu Hsi, and the square, as a 'terrestrial' symbol and therefore *yin* or feminine, to Niu Kua; but when they are represented together and joined by their serpent's tails (thus corresponding exactly to the two serpents of the caduceus), it is on the contrary Fu Hsi who holds the square and Niu Kua who holds the compasses.[13] This is explained in reality by an exchange comparable

9. The triangle here takes the place of the square, since, like it, it is a rectilinear figure, and this changes nothing of the symbolism in question.

10. Strictly speaking it is not a question here of the very terms so designated in the Great Triad, but of something that corresponds to them at a certain level and that is included within the manifested universe, as in the case of the *Tribhuvana*, but with this difference, that inasmuch as it represents the human state in its integrality it must be regarded as including both the Earth and the Atmosphere or 'intermediary region' of the *Tribhuvana*.

11. The celestial vault is the true 'canopy of perfection' referred to in certain grades of Scottish Freemasonry; we hope to be able in a separate study to examine the architectural symbolism related to this question.

12. *The Reign of Quantity and the Signs of the Times*, chap. 20.

13. On the other hand, such an inversion of attributes does not exist in depictions of the Hermetic *Rebis*, where the compasses are held by the masculine half, associated with the sun, and the square by the feminine half, associated with the moon. — On the subject of the correspondence between sun and moon, one might refer to what was said in an earlier note on the numbers 10 and 12, and also to the

to that mentioned above in regard to 'celestial' and 'terrestrial' numbers, an exchange which in such a case can be qualified quite properly as 'hierogamic';[14] without such an exchange it is hard to see how the compasses could belong to Niu Kua, all the more in that the actions attributed to her represent her as especially exercising the function of assuring the world's stability,[15] a function very much related to the 'substantial' side of manifestation, and that stability is expressed by the shape of the cube.[16] On the other hand, in a certain sense the square does indeed belong to Fu Hsi as 'Lord of the Earth', which he measures by it,[17] and under this aspect he corresponds to the 'Worshipful Master who rules by the square' in Masonic symbolism;[18] but if this is so, it is because, in himself and no longer in his relation with Niu Kua, he is *yin-yang* as being reintegrated into the state and the nature of 'primordial man'. From this new relationship the square itself takes on another meaning, for from the fact that it is formed of two rectilinear arms it can be regarded as the union of the horizontal and the vertical, which in one of their meanings, correspond respectively as we have already seen to Earth

words of the Emerald Tablet: 'The Sun is its father, the Moon its mother,' which relate precisely to the *Rebis* or 'Androgyne', this being the 'sole thing' where the 'virtues of Heaven and Earth' are gathered; 'sole', of course, in its essence, although double, *res bina*, as to its outward aspects, like the cosmic force which we spoke of earlier, and which in depictions of Fu Hsi and Niu Kua are symbolically recalled by the serpents' tails.

14. Granet expressly acknowledges this exchange between the compasses and the square (*La Pensée chinoise*, p363), as well as between odd and even numbers; this should have enabled him to avoid the awkward error of describing the compasses as a 'feminine emblem', as he does elsewhere (p267, note).

15. See *The Reign of Quantity and the Signs of the Times*, chap. 25.

16. This reversal of attributes between Fu Hsi and Niu Kua can be linked with the fact that in the third and fourth arcana of the Tarot, a celestial symbolism (stars) is attributed to the Empress and a terrestrial symbolism (cubic stone) to the Emperor; moreover, numerically and by rank, the Empress is associated with the number 3, which is odd, and the Emperor with 4, an even number, which also produces the same inversion.

17. We will return to this measuring of the Earth in connection with the layout of the *Ming T'ang*.

18. The Empire organized and governed by Fu Hsi and his successors was constituted, like the Masonic Lodge, in such a way as to be an image of the Cosmos in its totality.

and Heaven, as well as to *yin* and *yang* in all their applications; and this is moreover why, again in Masonic symbolism, the square of the 'Worshipful Master' is considered as the union or synthesis of the level and the perpendicular.[19]

We will add one final observation concerning the representations of Fu Hsi and Niu Kua: the first is placed on the left and the second on the right,[20] which indeed corresponds to the pre-eminence that the Far-Eastern tradition usually attributes to the left over the right and which we explained earlier.[21] At the same time, Fu Hsi holds the square in his left hand while Niu Kua holds the compasses in her right; here, because of the respective meanings of the compasses and the square in themselves, the saying we have already quoted should be remembered: 'The Way of Heaven prefers the right; the Way of Earth prefers the left.'[22] In an example such as this it can thus be seen very clearly that traditional symbolism is always perfectly coherent, but also that it could never lend itself to any more or less narrow 'systematization' since it must answer to the multitude of diverse points of view from which things can be envisaged, and it is because of this that it opens up possibilities of conception that are truly unlimited.

19. The level and the perpendicular are also the respective attributes of the two Wardens and are thereby directly related to the two terms of the complementarism represented by the two pillars of the Temple of Solomon. — It is also worth noting that whereas Fu Hsi's square seems to have arms of equal length, that of the Worshipful Master on the contrary regularly has unequal arms; this difference may correspond in a general way to the shapes of a square and a more or less elongated rectangle; but in addition the inequality of the arms of the square refers more precisely to the 'secret' of Operative Masonry concerning the formation of a right triangle whose sides are respectively proportional to the numbers 3, 4, and 5, a triangle whose symbolism we shall meet again later.

20. In this case it is naturally a question of the right and left sides of the figures themselves, and not those of the observer.

21. In the figure of the *Rebis* the masculine half is on the contrary at the right and the feminine half at the left; moreover, the figure has only two hands, the right holding the compasses and the left the square.

22. *Chou Li.*

16

THE *MING T'ANG*

Toward the end of the third millennium BC, China was divided into nine provinces[1] arranged geometrically as in the following diagram (figure 16): one at the center and eight at the four cardinal points and the four intermediate points. This arrangement is attributed by tradition to Yü the Great (*Ta Yü*),[2] who, as the story goes, traveled over the world to 'measure the Earth'; and since this measurement was carried out in the shape of a square, we see here the use of the square attributed to the Emperor as 'Lord of the Earth'.[3] He was inspired to this division into nine by the diagram called *Lo Chu* or 'Writing of the Lake' which according to legend was brought to him by a

4	9	2
3	5	7
8	1	6

Figure 16

---

1. The territory of China was apparently contained at that time between the Yellow River and the Blue River.

2. It is at least curious to note the singular resemblance between the name and title of Yü the Great and those of *Hu Gadarn* in Celtic tradition; should we suppose from this that they are something like secondary and particular 'localizations' of one and the same 'prototype', which goes back much further, perhaps even to the primordial tradition itself? This parallel is no more extraordinary moreover than those we have referred to elsewhere on the subject of the 'island of the four Masters' visited by Emperor Yao, the very same Emperor whom Yü the Great originally served as minister (see *The King of the World*, chap. 9).

3. This square has arms of equal length as we have said because the shape of the Empire itself and that of its divisions were regarded as perfect squares.

tortoise[4] and in which the first nine numbers are arranged to form what is called a 'magic square';[5] in this way the Empire was made into an image of the Universe. In this 'magic square'[6] the center is occupied by the number 5, which is itself the 'middle' of the nine primary numbers,[7] and as we saw above it is indeed the 'central' number of Earth in the same way that 6 is the 'central' number of Heaven.[8] The central province, which corresponded to this number and where the Emperor resided, was called the 'Middle Kingdom' (*Chung Kuo*),[9] and it was from here that this name is thought to have been later extended to all of China. But in reality there is some doubt about this last point, for just as the 'Middle Kingdom' occupied a central position in the Empire, so from the beginning the whole Empire could be conceived as occupying a similar position in the world; and this indeed seems to result from the fact that it was

4. The other traditional diagram, called *Ho Tu* or 'River Scene', in which the numbers are arranged as a 'cross', is associated with Fu Hsi and the dragon in the same way that the *Lo Chu* is associated with Yü the Great and the tortoise.

5. We are obliged to retain this name since we have none better at our disposal, but it has the disadvantage of indicating only a very specialized usage (in connection with the making of talismans) of numerical squares of this kind, whose essential characteristic is that the numbers contained all the vertical and horizontal lines, as well as the two diagonals, always yielding the same sum, which in this particular case is 15.

6. If instead of numbers we place the *yin-yang* symbol (figure 9) at the center and the eight *kua* or trigrams in the other regions, we have in a square or 'terrestrial' form the equivalent of the circular or 'celestial' diagram where the *kua* are usually laid out, either in the arrangement of the 'primary Heaven' (*shen T'ien*) attributed to Fu Hsi, or in the arrangement of the 'secondary Heaven' (*kou T'ien*) attributed to Wen Wang.

7. The product of 5 and 9 is 45, which is also the sum of all the nine numbers in the square whose center is the number 5.

8. Let us recall in this connection that $5 + 6 = 11$ expresses the 'central union of Heaven and Earth'. — In the square, the pairs of opposite numbers all have as sum $10 = 5 \times 2$. It can also be noted that the odd or *yang* numbers are placed at the middle of each of the sides (the cardinal points), forming a cross (dynamic aspect), and that the even or *yin* numbers are placed at the corners (intermediary points), demarcating the square itself (static aspect).

9. Compare the Kingdom of *Mide*, or of the 'Middle', in ancient Ireland; but the latter was surrounded by only four other kingdoms, corresponding to the four cardinal points (see *The King of the World*, chap. 9).

constituted, as we just said, so as to form an image of the Universe. Indeed, the fundamental meaning of this fact is that everything is really contained in the center, so that everything in the entire Universe must be found there is some way and in 'archetype', if one may so express it. There could thus have been, on an ever more reduced scale, an entire series of similar[10] images, arranged concentrically and culminating finally at the central point itself where the Emperor resided,[11] who, as we said earlier, occupied the position of 'true man' and fulfilled the function of 'mediator' between Heaven and Earth.[12]

There should be no surprise at the 'central' position assigned to the Chinese Empire in relation to the world as a whole, for in fact it is the same for every region where the spiritual center of a tradition was established. This center was in fact an emanation or reflection of the supreme spiritual center, that is to say of the center of the primordial tradition from which all regular traditional forms are derived by adaptation to particular circumstances of time and place, and consequently it constituted an image of that supreme center with which it was in a virtual sense identified.[13] That is why every region, whatever it was, that possessed such a spiritual center, was by that very fact a 'Holy Land' and as such was symbolically designated by names like 'Center of the World' or 'Heart of the World', which it indeed was for those belonging to the tradition of which it was the seat and for whom communication with the supreme spiritual center was possible through the secondary spiritual center

10. This word must be taken in the precise sense that the term 'similar figures' has in geometry.

11. This central point was not precisely *centrum in trigono centri*, to invoke a formula known in Western initiations, but rather, in an equivalent way, *centrum in quadrato centri*.

12. One can find other traditional examples of such a 'concentration' in successive stages, and we have given one belonging to the Hebrew Kabbalah: 'The Tabernacle of the Holiness of *Jehovah*, the residence of the *Shekinah*, is the Holy of Holies that is the heart of the Temple, which itself is the center of Zion (Jerusalem), just as Holy Zion is the center of the Land of Israel and as the Land of Israel is the center of the world' (cf. *The King of the World*, chap. 6, [citation from P. Vulliaud, *La Kabbale juive*, I, p 509]).

13. See *The King of the World*, and also *Perspectives on Initiation*, chap. 10.

corresponding to that tradition.[14] The place where this secondary center was established was meant to be, in the language of the Hebrew Kabbalah, the place of manifestation of the *Shekinah* or 'Divine Presence',[15] that is, in Far-Eastern terminology, the point where the 'Activity of Heaven' is directly reflected, which as we have seen is properly the 'Invariable Middle', determined by the meeting of the 'World Axis' with the domain of human possibilities;[16] and what is particularly important to note in this regard is that the *Shekinah* was always represented as 'Light', just as the 'World Axis' was, as we have already pointed out, symbolically assimilated to a 'luminous ray'.

We mentioned a short while ago that just as the Chinese Empire as a whole represented, by the way it was constituted and divided, an image of the Universe, so also there must have been a similar image in that center which was the Emperor's residence, and so in fact there was; this was the *Ming T'ang*, which some sinologists, seeing only its most outward aspect, have called the 'House of the Calendar', but whose name really means literally 'Temple of Light', which immediately relates to our most recent remarks.[17] The character *ming* is composed of two characters representing the sun and

14. We have just given an example [note 12 above] of such an identification with the 'Center of the World' in the case of the Land of Israel. Among other examples, one can also cite that of ancient Egypt: according to Plutarch, 'the Egyptians call their country Chemia [*Kemi*, or 'black earth', whence the word 'alchemy'] and compare it to a heart' (*Isis and Osiris*, chap. 33). Whatever geographical or other reasons for this comparison might have been given exoterically, in reality it is only justified by an assimilation to the true 'Heart of the World' [cf. *The King of the World*, chap. 6, and *Insights into Christian Esoterism*, chap. 3].

15. See *The King of the World*, chap. 3 and *The Symbolism of the Cross*, chap. 7. This is what the Temple of Jerusalem was for the Hebrew tradition, and this is why the Tabernacle or Holy of Holies was called *mishkan*, the 'divine abode'; the High Priest alone could enter it, to fulfill, as the Emperor in China, the function of 'mediator'.

16. The determination of a place capable of corresponding effectively to this 'Invariable Middle' essentially belonged to the traditional science which we have on other occasions referred to by the name 'sacred geography' [see *The King of the World*, chap. 11].

17. It is not out of place to compare the meaning of the name *Ming T'ang* to the identical meaning implicit in the word 'Lodge', as we have already noted elsewhere

the moon; it thus expresses light in its total manifestation, in both its direct and reflected modalities, for although light in itself is essentially *yang*, in order to manifest itself it must assume, like all things, two complementary aspects which are *yang* and *yin* with respect to each other and which correspond respectively to the sun and to the moon[18] since, in the domain of manifestation, *yang* is never without *yin* nor *yin* without *yang*.[19]

The plan of the *Ming T'ang* conformed to what we described above for the division of the Empire (figure 16), that is, it consisted of nine rooms arranged exactly as the nine provinces; however, instead of being perfect squares, the *Ming T'ang* and its rooms were more or less elongated rectangles the proportions of whose sides varied from dynasty to dynasty, just like the height of the chariot pole mentioned earlier, because of the different cyclic periods to

(*Perspectives on Initiation*, chap. 46), whence the Masonic expression 'a well-illuminated and ordered place' (cf. *The King of the World*, chap. 3). Moreover, both *Ming T'ang* and Lodge are images of the Cosmos (*Loka*, in the etymological sense of this Sanskrit term) considered as the domain or 'field' of manifestation of Light (cf. *The Reign of Quantity and the Signs of the Times*, chap. 3). — It is necessary to add here that the *Ming T'ang* is represented in the initiation sites of the *T'ien Ti Huei* (cf. B. Favre, *Les Sociétés secrètes en Chine*, pp138–9, and 170); one of the principal mottoes of this organization is 'Destroy darkness [*ching*], restore light [*ming*],' just as the Master Masons must work to 'spread the light and gather what is scattered.' The application of this by 'homophony' in modern times to the *Ming* and *Ch'ing* dynasties, represents only a contingent and temporary goal assigned to certain outward 'emanations' of this organization working in the domain of social and even political activity.

18. In the Hindu tradition these are the two eyes of *Vaishvānara*, which are associated respectively with the subtle currents of the right and the left, that is, with the two aspects, *yang* and *yin*, of the cosmic force we spoke of earlier (cf. *Man and His Becoming according to the Vedānta*, chaps. 13 and 21). The Far-Eastern tradition also designates them as the 'eye of day' and the 'eye of night', and it is hardly necessary to point out that day is *yang* and night *yin*.

19. We have already amply discussed the properly initiatic meaning of 'Light' in sufficient detail elsewhere (*Perspectives on Initiation*, especially chaps. 4, 46, and 47); in connection with Light and its 'central' manifestation, let us also recall here what was noted about the symbolism of the Blazing Star as a symbol of regenerated Man residing in the 'Middle' and placed between the square and the compasses, which like the base and the roof of the *Ming T'ang* correspond respectively to Earth and Heaven.

which these dynasties corresponded. We shall not enter here into details on this subject, for the principle alone is of importance now.[20] The *Ming T'ang* had twelve openings to the outside, three on each of its four sides, so that, although the rooms in the middle of each side had only one opening, those at the corner had two each. These twelve entrances corresponded to the twelve months of the year: those on the eastern facade to the three months of spring, those on the southern facade to the three months of summer, those on the western facade to the three months of autumn, and those on the northern facade to the three months of winter. The twelve entrances thus formed a zodiac,[21] and so corresponded exactly to the twelve gates of the 'Celestial Jerusalem' as described in the Apocalypse,[22] which is also the 'Center of the World' and an image of the Universe in both a spatial and a temporal sense.[23]

During the course of the annual cycle the Emperor completed a circumambulation within the *Ming T'ang* in the 'solar' direction (figure 14), placing himself successively at the twelve stations corresponding to the twelve openings, where he promulgated the ordinances (*yueh ling*) for the twelve months; in this way he identified himself successively with the 'twelve suns', which are the twelve *ādityas* of Hindu tradition, and also the 'twelve fruits of the Tree of Life' in Apocalyptic symbolism.[24] This circumambulation was always accomplished with a return to the center which marked the middle of the year,[25] just as, when visiting the Empire, he traveled

20. For these details one may refer to Granet, *La Pensée chinoise*, pp250–75. — The ritual of delimitation of an area such as that of the *Ming T'ang* was equivalent to the determination of a *templum* in the original and etymological sense of the word (cf. *Perspectives on Initiation* chap. 17).

21. This arrangement in a square represents properly speaking a terrestrial projection of the circular celestial zodiac.

22. Cf. *The King of the World*, chap. 11 and *The Reign of Quantity and the Signs of the Times*, chap. 20. — The plan of the 'Celestial Jerusalem' is also a square.

23. Moreover, time is 'changed into space' at the end of the cycle, so that all of its phases must then be envisaged in simultaneity (see *The Reign of Quantity and the Signs of the Times*, chap. 23).

24. Cf. *The King of the World*, chaps. 4 and 11, and *The Symbolism of the Cross*, chap. 9.

25. This middle of the year falls at the autumn equinox when the year begins at the spring equinox, as it generally does in the Far-Eastern tradition (although in

the provinces in a corresponding order and then returned to his central residence, and also as the sun itself, in Far-Eastern symbolism, after completing a cycle (whether of a day, a month, or a year), always returns to rest on its tree which, like the 'Tree of Life' at the center of the 'Terrestrial Paradise' and the 'Celestial Jerusalem', is a figuration of the 'World Axis'. It must be clear that the Emperor's role in all of this was properly that of 'regulator' of the cosmic order itself, which supposes moreover the union in him or by him of celestial and terrestrial influences, which, as we mentioned earlier, also correspond respectively in a certain way to the temporal and spatial determinations which the layout of the *Ming T'ang* put into direct relation with each other.

this regard there were changes at certain periods that must have corresponded to the changes of orientation which we spoke of above, something that is normal because of the geographical localization of that tradition, since the East corresponds to spring. Let us recall in this connection that the East-West axis is equinoctial whereas the North-South axis is solstitial.

17

WANG:
THE KING PONTIFF

THERE ARE STILL OTHER CONSIDERATIONS that must be developed in order to explain what the royal function was in the Far Eastern tradition, or at least what is usually translated as such, though in a way that is obviously inadequate, for if *Wang* is indeed King in the proper sense of the word, he is also something else at the same time. Moreover, this follows from the very symbolism of the character *wang* (figure 17), which is composed of three horizontal lines corresponding respectively, like the trigrams we spoke of earlier, to Heaven, Man, and Earth,

Figure 17

united at their centers by a vertical line, for, as the etymologists say, 'the function of the King is to unite,' by which is to be understood, because of the very position of the vertical line, to unite Heaven and Earth. What this character properly designates is therefore Man insofar as he is middle term of the Great Triad, and envisaged especially in his role as 'mediator'; in order to be yet more precise we should add that Man must not be considered here only as 'primordial man' but as indeed 'Universal Man' himself, for the vertical line is nothing other than the axis which effectively unites all states of existence, while the center where 'primordial man' is placed, which is marked in the character by the point where the vertical line intersects the middle horizontal line at the center of the latter, relates to only one state, which is the individual human state;[1] moreover, the part of the character that properly refer to Man, which includes the vertical line plus the middle horizontal line (since the upper and lower lines represent Heaven and Earth) form a cross, which is the very symbol of 'Universal Man'.[2] This identification of *Wang* with 'Universal Man' is further confirmed by texts such as this passage from Lao Tzu: 'The Way is great, Heaven is great; Earth is great; the King is also great. In the middle there are therefore four great things, but the King alone is visible.'[3]

If therefore the *Wang* is essentially 'Universal Man', the one who represents him and fulfills his function must be, at least in principle, a 'transcendent man', that is, have realized the final goal of the 'greater mysteries'; and it is as such that he can, as we indicated above, be effectively identified with the 'Middle Way' (*Chung Tao*), that is to say with the axis itself, whether that axis be represented by the pole of the chariot, by the central pillar of the *Ming T'ang*, or by any equivalent symbol. Having developed all his possibilities in the vertical as well as the horizontal directions, he is by that very fact the 'Lord of the Three Worlds',[4] which can also be represented by

---

1. Granet seems to have understood nothing about the relationship between axis and center, for he writes: 'The notion of the center is far from primitive; it was substituted for the idea of the axis' (*La Pensée chinoise*, p104). In reality, the two symbols have always coexisted, for they are in no way equivalent and therefore cannot be substituted for each other. This is a good example of the misunderstanding to which the prejudice of seeing everything 'historically' can lead.

2. For this reason we have represented the middle term of the Great Triad in figure 6 by this cross.

3. *Tao Te Ching*, chap. 25. — Let us note in passing that this text alone would suffice to refute the opinion of those orientalists who, taking everything in a 'material' sense and confusing the symbol with the thing symbolized, imagine that the Heaven and Earth of Far-Eastern tradition are nothing but the visible sky and the earth. [For the final phrase 'but of these only the King is visible', all current English translations have 'and the King is one of them'. ED.]

4. Cf. *The King of the World*, chap. 4. — If one wishes to point to parallels among different traditions, it can be noted that it is in this quality that Hermes, who is moreover represented as both 'king' and 'pontiff', is called *trismegistos*, or 'thrice-great'; this designation can also be linked with that of 'thrice-mighty' used in the 'grades of perfection' of Scottish Freemasonry, which implies the delegation of a power to be exercised in the Three Worlds.

the three horizontal lines of the character *wang*;[5] and with respect to the human world in particular he is also 'Unique Man' who synthesizes in himself and integrally expresses Humanity (envisaged at once as a specific nature, from the cosmic point of view, and as the collectivity of men from the social point of view), the same as Humanity in turn synthesizes in itself the 'ten thousand beings', that is, the totality of beings of this world.[6] This is why he is the 'regulator' of the cosmic order as well as the social order, as we have already seen;[7] and when he fulfills the function of 'mediator' it is really all men that fulfill it in his person; thus, in China, the *Wang* or Emperor alone was able to accomplish the public rites corresponding to that function, and especially to offer the sacrifice to Heaven which is the very type of these rites, for it is here that the role of 'mediator' is affirmed in the most evident way.[8]

Insofar as *Wang* is identified with the vertical axis it is designated as the 'Royal Way' (*Wang Tao*); but on the other hand, that same axis is also the 'Way of Heaven' (*T'ien Tao*), as can be seen from the figure (7) where the vertical and the horizontal respectively represent Heaven and Earth, so that in the final analysis the 'Royal Way' is identical with the 'Way of Heaven'.[9] Moreover, one is really *Wang*

---

5. For this a change of viewpoint is needed corresponding to what we explained earlier on the subject of the *Tribhuvana* in comparison to the Far-Eastern Triad.

6. It will be noted that the character of 'Lord of the Three Worlds' corresponds here to the vertical direction, while that of 'Unique Man' corresponds to the horizontal.

7. The word *rex*, 'king', expresses etymologically the 'regulatory' function, but ordinarily applied solely from the social point of view.

8. In fact, the sacrifice to Heaven is also offered within initiatic organizations, but once it is no longer a matter of a public rite there is no 'usurpation' in this fact; thus the emperors, when they themselves were initiates, could only adopt one attitude, which was simply to officially ignore those sacrifices, and this is indeed what they did; but when they were really no more than mere profane men, they sometimes tried to ban them, in vain, however, because they could not understand that others than themselves were effectively and 'personally' what they themselves were only symbolically by virtue of exercising the traditional function with which they had been invested.

9. Regarding the 'Way of Heaven', we will cite this passage from the *I Ching*: 'To establish the Way of Heaven: that is *yin* plus *yang*. To establish the Way of Earth: that is soft [*jou*] plus hard [*yo*]. To establish the Way of Man: that is humanity plus

only if he possesses the 'mandate of Heaven' (*T'ien ming*),[10] by virtue of which he is legitimately recognized as the Son of Heaven (*T'ien Tzu*);[11] and this mandate can only be received along the axis considered in its descending direction, that is, in the direction that is inverse and reciprocal to that along which the 'mediating' function will be exercised, because this is the sole and invariable direction in which the 'Activity of Heaven' is exercised. Now this presupposes, if not necessarily the quality of 'transcendent man', at the very least that of 'true man' actually residing in the 'Invariable Middle', for it is at this central point alone that the axis intersects the domain of the human state.[12]

According to a symbolism common to most traditions, this axis is also the 'bridge' that connects Earth to either Heaven, as here, or the human state to the supra-individual states, or even the sensible world to the suprasensible world; it is always the 'World Axis', but viewed sometimes in its entirety or only in one of its parts, of greater or lesser extent, according to the degree of universality in which this symbolism is taken in different cases. From this it can be seen that this 'bridge' must be understood as essentially vertical,[13]

---

justice'. This, applied to the three terms of the Great Triad, is the neutralization and unification of complementaries, by which the return to principial indistinction is achieved. — It is worth noting that the two complementaries that relate to Man coincide exactly with the two lateral pillars of the Sephirothic Tree in the Kabbalah: Mercy and Rigor.

10. The word *ming*, 'mandate', is a homophone for the word meaning 'light', as well as for other words meaning 'name' and 'destiny'. — 'The power of the Sovereign derives from the power of the Principle; his person is chosen by Heaven' (*Chuang Tzu*, chap. 12).

11. One may refer to what we have said earlier about Man as 'Son of Heaven and Earth'.

12. It is moreover acknowledged that the 'mandate of Heaven' can only be received directly by the founder of a dynasty, who then transmits it to his successors; but if they should come to lose it because of a lack of 'qualification' resulting from a degeneration, this dynasty must come to an end and be replaced by another. Thus in each dynasty there is a downward trajectory which, at its degree of localization in time and space, corresponds in a certain way to that of the great cycles of terrestrial humanity.

13. Cf. *as-ṣirāṭ al-mustaqīm* in the Islamic tradition (see *The Symbolism of the Cross*, chap. 25); one could also cite among other examples the bridge *Chinwat* of Mazdaism.

and this is an important point to which we will perhaps return in another study.[14] In this aspect the *Wang* is properly *Pontifex* in the strictly etymological sense of the word;[15] more precisely still, because of another identification with the axis he is both 'bridge builder' and 'bridge' itself; and one could further say that this 'bridge', by which communication with the higher states, and through them with the Principle itself, is made possible, can only be truly established by one who is himself effectively identified with it. This is why we think that the expression 'King-Pontiff' is the only one that can adequately render the word *Wang*, for it is the only one that fully describes the function it implies; and thus it can be seen that this function has a double aspect, for in reality it is both a sacerdotal and a royal function.[16]

This is moreover easy to understand, for even if the *Wang* is not actually a 'transcendent man' as he should be in principle, but only a 'true man' who has arrived at the term of the 'lesser mysteries', he is by virtue of the 'central' position he thereupon occupies effectively beyond any distinction of spiritual and temporal powers. He could even be described as 'anterior' in terms of 'cyclical' symbolism to this distinction, for he has been reintegrated into the 'primordial state', where no special function is yet differentiated but

---

14. See *Symbols of Sacred Science*, chaps. 63 and 64. ED.

15. Cf. *Spiritual Authority and Temporal Power*, chap. 4.

16. It could be asked why we do not rather say 'Pontiff-King', which would doubtless seem more logical at first glance since the 'pontifical' or sacerdotal function is by its very nature higher than the royal function, and its pre-eminence would thus be marked by naming it first. If we nonetheless prefer the expression 'King-Pontiff', this is because by stating the royal before the sacerdotal function (which is commonly done without thought when one speaks of the 'King-Mage'), we follow the traditional order of which we spoke in connection with the term *yin-yang*, where the 'outward' is expressed before the 'inward', for the royal function is obviously more outward than the sacerdotal function; besides, in relation to each other, the priesthood is *yang* and royalty is *yin*, as Ananda K. Coomaraswamy has shown so well in his book *Spiritual Authority and Temporal Power in the Indian Theory of Government*, and as is also indicated in the symbolism of the keys by the respectively vertical and horizontal positions of the keys representing these two functions, as well as by the fact that the first is made of gold, corresponding to the sun, and the second of silver, corresponding to the moon.

which contains in itself the possibilities corresponding to all functions by the very fact that it represents the integral plenitude of the human state.[17] In every case, and even when he is only symbolically 'Unique Man', whom he represents by virtue of the 'mandate of Heaven',[18] he is the very source or common principle of those two powers, a principle from which the spiritual authority and sacerdotal function derive directly and the temporal power and royal function derive indirectly through their mediation. This principle can indeed be properly called 'heavenly', and from it, through the priesthood and the royalty, the spiritual influences descend gradually along the axis, first to the 'intermediary world', then to the terrestrial world itself.[19]

Thus, once the *Wang*, having received the 'mandate of Heaven' either directly or indirectly, is identified with the axis considered in its ascending aspect, either, in the first case, effectively and in himself (and we recall here the rites representing this ascension which we mentioned previously), or, in the second, virtually and only by the accomplishment of his function (and it is obvious that a rite, for example, such as the sacrifice to Heaven, acts in an 'ascending' direction), he becomes so to speak the 'channel' through which the influences descend from Heaven toward Earth.[20] In the action of these spiritual influences we see a double, alternating movement, in turn

17. Cf. *Spiritual Authority and Temporal Power*, chap. 1, and also, on the 'return' of the cycle to the 'primordial state' in the 'lesser mysteries', *Perspectives on Initiation*, chap. 39.

18. He thus possesses this mandate by transmission, as we indicated earlier, and it is this that allows him when exercising his function to hold the place of 'true man' and even of 'transcendent man', although he has not 'personally' realized the corresponding states. — There is something here comparable to the transmission of the spiritual influence or *barakah* in Islamic initiatic organizations: by this transmission a *khalifah* can take the place of the *Shaykh* and validly fulfill his function without however actually having attained to the *Shaykh*'s own spiritual state.

19. Cf. *Spiritual Authority and Temporal Power*, chap. 4.

20. In speaking here of a 'channel', we are alluding to a symbolism that is found expressly in various traditions; in this connection let us recall not only the *nāḍīs* or 'channels' by which, according to the Hindu tradition, the currents of subtle force circulate in the human being, but also and above all the Sephirothic tree in the Hebrew Kabbalah, by which, precisely, spiritual influences spread and communicate from one world to another.

ascending and descending, to which corresponds, at the lower level of psychic or subtle influences, the double current of the cosmic force mentioned above; but we must be careful to note that, as concerns spiritual influences, the movement takes place along the axis itself or the 'Middle Way', for as the *I Ching* says, 'the Way of Heaven is *yin* with *yang*,' and the two complementary aspects are then inseparably united in this same 'central' direction, while in the psychic domain, which is further from the principial order, the differentiation of *yang* and *yin* determines the production of two distinct currents, represented by the different symbols of which we have already spoken, and which can be described as occupying respectively the 'right' and 'left' of the 'Middle Way'.[21]

21. The 'Middle Way' corresponds at the 'microcosmic' level to the 'subtle' artery *sushumnā* of Hindu tradition, which terminates in the *Brahmārandhra* (represented by the point where the chariot pole emerges from the canopy, or where the central pillar of the *stūpa* emerges from the dome), and at the 'macrocosmic' level to the 'solar ray', also called *sushumnā*, and with which this artery is in constant communication. The two contrary currents of the cosmic force have as their corresponding features in the human being, as we have already said, the *nāḍis* of the right and left, *iḍā* and *piṅgalā* (cf. *Man and His Becoming according to the Vedānta*, chap. 20). — One can also make a comparison with the distinction of the two Tantric 'ways' of the right and left, which we spoke about in connection with the *vajra* and which, being represented by a simple tilting of the axial symbol in one direction or another, are thus seen to really be only secondary specifications of the 'Middle Way'.

18

TRUE MAN AND
TRANSCENDENT MAN

IN THE FOREGOING we have continually spoken of 'true man' and 'transcendent man', but we must make some further complementary distinctions here, and the first point to be made is that while 'true man' (*chen jen*) has been called by some 'transcendent man', such a designation is rather inappropriate, for 'true man' has only reached the fullness of the human state, and only what is above this state can be truly called 'transcendent'. That is why it is proper to reserve the title 'transcendent man' to he who is sometimes called 'divine man' or 'spiritual man' (*shen jen*), that is, anyone who, having arrived at total realization and the 'Supreme Identity', is no longer properly speaking a man in the individual sense of that word, since he has passed beyond humanity and is entirely freed from its specific conditions[1] as well as from all the other limiting conditions of any state of existence whatsoever.[2] He has thus effectively become 'Universal Man', whereas this is not so for 'true man', who is only identified in fact with 'primordial man'; however, it can be said that 'true man' is already at least virtually 'Universal Man', in the sense that since he no longer has to traverse other states in distinctive mode—having passed from the circumference to the center[3]—the human state will

1. We will refer here to what was said above about this point in connection with the relationship of the being and the environment.

2. 'In the body of a man he is no longer a man.... Infinitely small [the 'trace' which we will speak of below] is that which makes him still a man; infinitely great is that which makes him one with Heaven': *Chuang Tzu*, chap. 5.

3. Buddhism expresses this by the term *anāgamī*, that is, 'he who returns not' to another state of manifestation (cf. *Perspectives on Initiation*, chap. 39).

necessarily be for him the central state of the total being, although not yet in an effective way.[4]

'Transcendent man' and 'true man', corresponding respectively to the terms of the 'greater mysteries' and the 'lesser mysteries', are the two highest grades in the Taoist hierarchy; this also contains three lower grades,[5] which naturally represent different stages on the way of the 'lesser mysteries',[6] and which are in descending order the 'man of the Way', that is, he who is on the Way (*Tao jen*), the 'man of talent' (*chu jen*), and the 'wise man' (*cheng jen*), whose wisdom, though something more than mere 'learning', is still only of an outward order. Indeed, this lowest degree of the Taoist hierarchy coincides with the highest degree of the Confucian hierarchy, thus establishing continuity between them, which is in conformity with the normal relationship of Taoism and Confucianism insofar as they are respectively the esoteric and the exoteric side of the same tradition; thus the first has its starting-point exactly where the second stops. The Confucian hierarchy for its part consists of three grades, which are in ascending order the 'man of letters' (*chu*),[7] the 'learned man' (*hsien*), and the 'wise man' (*cheng*); and it is said: 'The *chu* looks to [that is, takes as model] the *hsien*, the *hsien* looks to the *cheng*, and the *cheng* looks to Heaven,' for, from the boundary-point between the exoteric and the esoteric domains where the last is situated, everything above him is as it were confounded in his perspective with Heaven itself.

This last point is particularly important because it allows us to understand how there can be confusion between the roles of 'transcendent man' and 'true man'. This is not only because, as we just said, the latter is virtually what the first is effectively, nor because there is a certain correspondence between the 'lesser mysteries' and

---

4. Cf. *The Symbolism of the Cross*, chap. 28.

5. These degrees are mentioned particularly in a Taoist text dating to the fourth or fifth century AD (*Wen Tzu* 7:18).

6. It is worth mentioning, on the other hand, that the possible stages of attainment in the 'greater mysteries' are not distinctly set forth, because in terms of human language they are strictly speaking 'indescribable'.

7. This degree includes the entire hierarchy of official functions, which therefore correspond only to what is most external in the exoteric order itself.

the 'greater mysteries' that in Hermetic symbolism is represented by the analogy between the operations leading to 'whitening' and 'reddening'; there is something more. This is that the only point on the axis that is situated in the domain of the human state is the center of that state, so that for anyone who has not reached this center the axis itself is not directly perceptible, but only by the point that is its 'trace' on the plane representing that domain; this comes back in other words to what we have already said, that since direct communication with the higher states of the being is achieved along the axis, it is only possible from the center; as for the rest of the human domain, there can only be an indirect communication by a sort of refraction from this center. Thus, on the one hand, the being established at the center without being identified with the axis can really play the same role of 'mediator' with respect to the human state that 'Universal Man' plays for the totality of states; and on the other hand, he who has gone beyond the human state by rising up the axis to the higher states is by that very fact 'lost to view', so to speak, for all those who are in that state and have not yet reached its center, including those who possess effective initiatic degrees, though degrees lower than that of 'true man'. The latter then have no means of distinguishing 'transcendent man' from 'true man', for from the human state 'transcendent man' can only be perceived by his 'trace',[8] and that 'trace' is identical with the figure of 'true man'; from this point of view the one is thus really indistinguishable from the other.

Thus, in the eyes of ordinary men, and even in the eyes of initiates who have not yet completed the 'lesser mysteries', not only 'transcendent man' but also 'true man' appears as the 'agent' or representative of Heaven, which as it were manifests itself to them through him, for his action, or rather his influence, by the very fact that it is 'central' (and here the axis is not distinct from the center which is its 'trace'), imitates, as we have already explained, the 'Activity of Heaven', and 'incarnates' it so to speak with respect to the human world. This influence, being 'non-acting', implies no

---

8. This 'trace' is what would be called in Western traditional terminology *vestigium pedis*; we only mention this point in passing, for it involves an entire symbolism that would require a fuller treatment of its own.

outward activity; the 'Unique Man', exercising from the center the function of 'unmoved mover', orders all things without intervening in any of them, just as the Emperor, without ever leaving the *Ming T'ang*, controls all the regions of the Empire and regulates the course of the annual cycle, for 'To be concentrated in non-action, that is the Way of Heaven.'[9]

> The sovereigns of old, abstaining from any action of their own, allowed Heaven to govern through them.... At the summit of the universe the Principle exerts its influence over Heaven and Earth, which transmit that influence to all beings and, having become in the world of men good government, it causes talents and abilities to flourish. Inversely, all prosperity comes from good government whose efficacity derives from the Principle through the intermediary of Heaven and Earth. This is why, the sovereigns of old desiring nothing, the world was filled with abundance;[10] they did not act, and all things changed according to the norm;[11] they remained sunk in their meditation, and the people behaved with the most perfect order. This is what the ancient saying sums up thus: For him who unites himself to Unity, all things prosper; to him who has no desire of his own, even the genii are obedient.[12]

We must understand, therefore, that from the human point of view no distinction can be seen between 'transcendent man' and 'true man' (although there is really no common measure between them, any more than between the axis and one of its points), since what differentiates them is precisely what lies beyond the human state, so that if 'transcendent man' manifests himself in this state (or rather in relation to that state, for it is obvious that this manifestation in

---

9. *Chuang Tzu*, chap. 11.

10. There is something comparable to this in the Western idea of the Emperor as Dante conceived him, who saw in 'cupidity' the initial vice of all bad government (cf. especially *Convito* IV:4).

11. Similarly, in the Hindu tradition the *Chakravartî* or 'universal monarch' is literally 'he who turns the wheel' without himself participating in its movement.

12. *Chuang Tzu*, chap. 12.

no way implies a 'return' to the limiting conditions of human individuality), 'transcendent man' cannot appear here otherwise than as a 'true man'.[13] Of course it is no less true that between the total and unconditioned state of 'transcendent man', who is identical with 'Universal Man', and any conditioned state whatsoever, whether individual or supra-individual, and however lofty it may be, there can be no comparison when they are considered as they really are in themselves; but here we speak only of appearances from the point of view of the human state. Moreover, in a more general way, and with regard to all levels of the spiritual hierarchy, which are nothing else than hierarchies of effective initiation, it is only through the degree immediately above that each degree can perceive indistinctly all that is above it and receive its influences; and naturally those who have attained a certain degree can always (if they so wish and if the need arises) 'situate' themselves at any degree below their own without being at all affected by this apparent 'descent', for they possess *a fortiori* and 'eminently' so to speak all the corresponding states, which in the final analysis are for them only so many accidental or contingent 'functions'.[14] It is true that in the human world the 'transcendent man' can fulfill what is properly the function of 'true man', while on the other hand and inversely, 'true man' is for this same world as it were the representative or 'substitute' of 'transcendent man'.

---

13. This may serve to explain what we said elsewhere about the Sufis and the Rosicrucians (*Perspectives on Initiation* chap. 38).

14. Cf. *The Multiple States of the Being*, chap. 13. — 'In every hierarchic constitution, the higher orders possess the light and faculties of the lower orders, without these reciprocally having their perfection' (Dionysius the Areopagite, *The Celestial Hierarchy*, chap. 5).

19

DEUS
HOMO
NATURA

WE WILL ALSO COMPARE to the Far-Eastern Great Triad another ternary which was originally among traditional Western conceptions as they existed in the Middle Ages, and which is known even in the exoteric and merely 'philosophical' order; this ternary is usually expressed in the formula *Deus, Homo, Natura*. These three terms are generally regarded as the objects of the different kinds of knowledge that, in the language of Hinduism, are called 'non-supreme', that is, in sum, all that is not pure and transcendent metaphysical knowledge. Here, the middle term, Man, is clearly the same as in the Great Triad; but it remains to be seen in what way and to what extent the two other terms, God and Nature, correspond respectively to Heaven and Earth.

It must be noted at the outset that God in this context cannot be envisaged as the Principle as it is in itself, for this, being beyond all distinction, cannot enter into correlation with anything whatever, and the very way in which the ternary is presented implies a certain correlation, even a kind of complementarism, between God and Nature; this is therefore necessarily a point of view that can be called 'immanent' rather than 'transcendent' with respect to the Cosmos, of which these two terms are like the two poles; and even if they are outside manifestation, they cannot be considered distinctly except from its point of view. Moreover, among that collection of knowledge that is designated by the general term 'philosophy', in the ancient meaning of this word, God is the object only of what used to be called 'rational theology' to distinguish it from 'revealed theology', which in truth is indeed still 'non-supreme' but at least represents the knowledge of the Principle in the exoteric and specifically religious order, that is, in the measure this is possible taking into account both the inherent limitations of the corresponding domain and the special forms of expression that the truth must assume to adapt to this particular point of view. Now what is 'rational', that is, whatever relates exclusively to the exercise of individual human faculties, can obviously never in any way reach the Principle itself and, under the most favorable conditions,[1] can grasp only its relationship to the Cosmos.[2] From this it is easy to see that, save for the difference in points of view that must always be taken into consideration in such a case, this coincides precisely with what is designated by the Far-Eastern tradition as Heaven, since according to this tradition the Principle can be reached from the manifest universe only through Heaven,[3] for 'Heaven is the instrument of the Principle.'[4]

---

1. These conditions are realized in the case of an authentic traditional exoterism, as opposed to purely profane conceptions such as those of modern philosophy.

2. This is of course a relationship of the subordination of the Cosmos with respect to the Principle, and not a relationship of correlation; it is worth stressing this point so as to avoid even the slightest appearance of contradiction with what we said above.

3. This is why from the 'perspective' of manifestation the Principle appears as the 'pinnacle of Heaven' (*T'ien Chi*), as we have remarked before. — It is rather curious to note that when Christian missionaries want to translate the word 'God' into Chinese they always render it either as *T'ien* or *Chang Ti*, 'the Sovereign on high', which is the same thing as Heaven under another name. This would seem to indicate, probably without their being clearly aware of it, that for them the 'theological' point of view itself, in the most proper and complete sense, really did not reach as far as the Principle; moreover, they were no doubt wrong in this, but in any case they thereby show the true limitations of their own mentality and their inability to distinguish the different meanings that the word 'God' can have in Western languages for lack of more precise terms such as those found in the Eastern traditions. — On the subject of *Chang Ti* we cite this text: 'Heaven and Sovereign: it is all one. One says Heaven in speaking of his being; one says Sovereign in speaking of his government. Because it is so immense, his being is called Splendid Heaven; because the seat of his government is above, he is called Sublime Sovereign' (Commentary of *Chou Li*).

4. *Chuang Tzu*, chap. 11.

On the other hand, if one understands Nature in its primary sense, that is, as the primordial and undifferentiated Nature which is the root of all things (the *Mūlaprakṛiti* of the Hindu tradition), it goes without saying that it is identical with the Earth of the Far-Eastern tradition; but what introduces a complication is that, when Nature is spoken of as an object of knowledge, it is usually taken in a less strict and more extended sense than this, as the object of the study of all that can be called 'manifested nature', that is, everything that makes up the very totality of the cosmos.[5] This extension could be justified up to a certain point by saying that nature is envisaged in its 'substantial' rather than its 'essential' aspect, or that, as in the Hindu *Sāṅkhya* system, all things are considered as productions of *Prakriti*, setting aside the influence of *Purusha*, without which however nothing whatever can be effectively produced since it is obvious that from pure potentiality alone nothing can pass from potency to act; indeed, perhaps there is in this way of envisaging things a character inherent in the very viewpoint of 'physics' or 'natural philosophy'.[6] However, a more complete justification can be drawn from the remark that the totality of the cosmic environment is regarded as forming for Man his 'outer' world. This is only a matter of a mere change of level, so to speak, corresponding more appropriately to the human point of view, for everything that is exterior can at least in a relative fashion be described as 'terrestrial', just as all that is 'inner' can be called 'celestial'. It is also worth recalling here our earlier remarks about Sulphur, Mercury, and Salt: whatever is 'divine', being 'inner',[7] acts with respect to man like a

---

5. The use in Western languages of the one word 'nature' in both of these senses, though unavoidable, unfortunately does not fail to give rise to certain confusions; in Arabic, Primordial Nature is *al-Fiṭrah*, whereas manifested nature is *aṭ-ṭabī'ah*.

6. The word 'physics' is here taken in its ancient and etymological sense of 'science of nature' in general; but in English the expression 'natural philosophy', which was originally synonymous with it, has for a while in modern times, at least back to Newton, also served to designate 'physics' in the restricted and 'specialized' meaning in which it is ordinarily understood in our time.

7. In this connection let us recall the Gospel's *Regnum Dei intra vos est* [The Kingdom of God is within you].

'sulphurous' principle,[8] whereas whatever is 'natural', constituting the 'ambience', plays by that very fact the role of the 'mercurial' principle, as we explained when speaking of the relationship of the being with its environment. Man, product of both the 'divine' and of 'nature', finds himself placed, like Salt, at the common limit of the 'inner' and the 'outer', that is, at the point where celestial and terrestrial influences meet and balance each other.[9]

God and Nature, envisaged thus as correlatives or complementaries (and of course we must not lose sight of our initial remarks on the limited sense in which the term 'God' must be understood here in order to avoid on the one hand all 'pantheism', and on the other all 'association' in the sense of the Arabic word *shirk*),[10] appear respectively as the active principle and the passive principle of manifestation, or as 'act' and 'potency' in the Aristotelian sense of these terms: pure act and pure potency with respect to the totality of universal manifestation,[11] and relative act and relative potency with respect to every other more determined and more restricted level, that is, in the final analysis, always 'essence' and 'substance' in the different acceptations that we have explained on many occasions. To mark this respectively active and passive character the expressions *Natura naturans* and *Natura naturata*[12] are also used in a similar

8. Here again we find the double meaning ['sulphur' and 'divine'] of the Greek word *theion*.

9. Naturally, these considerations (which are properly speaking Hermetic) go far beyond simple exoteric philosophy; but this, precisely because it is exoteric, needs to be justified by something that goes beyond it.

10. It is on account of this sense that 'God' and 'Nature' are found inscribed in a symmetrical fashion on the symbols belonging to the 14th degree of Scottish Freemasonry.

11. It can be seen from this that the well-known definition of God as 'pure act' really applies not to Being itself, as some people believe, but only to the active pole of manifestation; in Far-Eastern terms, one would say that it is related to *T'ien*, and not to *T'ai Chi*.

12. Historians of philosophy generally attribute these expressions to Spinoza, but this is incorrect, for although it is true that he used them (adapting them, moreover, to fit his own particular conceptions), he is certainly not their author, and they really go back much further. — When one speaks of *Natura* without further specification, it is almost always *Natura naturata* that is meant, although

way, where the term *Natura*, instead of applying only to the passive principle as before, designates at once and symmetrically the two immediate principles of 'becoming'.[13] Here again we rejoin the Far-Eastern tradition, for which it is by *yang* and *yin*, and thus by Heaven and Earth, that all beings are modified, and in the manifested world 'the revolution of the principles *yin* and *yang* [corresponding to the reciprocal actions and reactions of the celestial and terrestrial influences] governs all things.'[14]

Once the two modalities of being [*yin-yang*] were differentiated within primordial Being [*T'ai Chi*], their revolution began and the Cosmos was modified accordingly. The apogee of *yin* [condensed in the Earth] is tranquil passivity; the apogee of *yang* [condensed in Heaven] is fecund activity. The passivity of Earth offers itself to Heaven, the activity of Heaven exercises itself on Earth, and the two give birth to all beings. An invisible force, the action and reaction of the binomial Heaven-Earth, produces every modification. Beginning and ending, fullness and emptiness,[15] astronomical revolutions [temporal cycles], phases of the sun [seasons] and of the moon, all these are produced by that single cause that nobody perceives but which always functions. Life moves toward a goal, death is a return toward a term. Generations and dissolutions [condensations and dissipations] succeed one another ceaselessly, without anyone knowing their origin, without anyone perceiving their end [both origin and end being

---

sometimes this term can also include both *Natura naturans* and *Natura naturata*; in this last case it has no correlation because there is nothing else apart from it besides the Principle on the one hand and manifestation on the other, whereas in the first case it is properly the *Natura* of the ternary that we just envisaged.

13. The essential idea of the Latin *natura*, like its Greek equivalent *physis*, is 'becoming'; manifested nature is 'what becomes'; the principles involved are 'what causes to become'.

14. *Lieh Tzu*.

15. Properly speaking, the allusion here is to 'emptiness of form' that is, to the non-formal state.

concealed in the Principle]. The action and reaction of Heaven and Earth are the sole motor behind this movement,[16]

which through an indefinite series of modifications leads beings to the final 'transformation' that brings them back to the one Principle from which they issued.[17]

16. *Chuang Tzu*, chap. 21.
17. This is the 'departure from the Cosmos' to which we alluded in connection with the extremity of the pole protruding above the chariot canopy.

20

DISTORTIONS IN
MODERN PHILOSOPHY

AT THE BEGINNING OF MODERN PHILOSOPHY Bacon still considered the three terms *Deus*, *Homo*, and *Natura* to be three distinct
objects of knowledge, to which he related the three great divisions
of 'philosophy'; however, he attributed a preponderant importance
to 'natural philosophy' or the science of nature in conformity with
the 'experimentalist' tendency of the modern mentality, which he
represented for that time, just as Descartes for his part represented
especially its 'rationalist' tendency.[1] But this was still largely a matter of 'proportion';[2] it was left to the nineteenth century for an
extraordinary and unprecedented deformation concerning this
same ternary to appear: we are referring to the so-called 'law of the
three estates' of Auguste Comte. But as the connection between this
and the ternary in question may not be evident at first glance, a few
words on this subject will perhaps not be without usefulness, for
this is a rather curious example of how the modern mind can dena-
ture information of traditional origin once it decides to appropriate
it rather than simply rejecting it.

Comte's fundamental error in this regard was to imagine that no
matter what type of speculation man undertakes, he has never

1. Descartes also devotes himself principally to 'physics', although he claims to
establish it by deductive reasoning on the model of mathematics, whereas Bacon on
the contrary wishes to establish it on an entirely experimental basis.
2. Apart, of course, from the reservations that could be made regarding the
entirely profane manner in which the sciences were already being conceived; but we
are speaking here only of the recognized object of knowledge, independently of the
point of view from which it is envisaged.

intended anything more than the explanation of natural phenomena. Starting from this narrow point of view, he is inevitably led to suppose that all knowledge, of no matter what order, is merely a more or less imperfect attempt to explain these phenomena. Joining this preconception to a wholly fantastic view of history, he believes that he has discovered in the different kinds of knowledge that have actually existed three types of explanation that he considers to be successive, because, wrongly relating them to the same object, he naturally finds them incompatible with each other. He therefore associates them with three distinct phases which the human mind must have passed through over the centuries, which he calls respectively the 'theological state', the 'metaphysical state', and the 'positive state'. In the first phase, the occurrence of phenomena is attributed to the intervention of supernatural agents; in the second, these phenomena are associated with natural forces, inherent in things and no longer transcendent with respect to them; lastly, the third phase is characterized by renouncing the search for 'causes', which is replaced by the search for 'laws', that is, constant relationships between phenomena. This final state, which Comte, moreover, regards as the sole definitively valid one, quite accurately represents the relative and limited standpoint of the modern sciences; all that he says concerning the two other 'states' is really nothing but a mass of confusion; it would be of little interest to examine it in detail, and we will simply take those points that bear directly on the question at hand.

Comte claims that in each phase the various elements of each kind of explanation were gradually coordinated, to finally culminate in the idea of a unique principle that includes them all; thus in the 'theological state', the different supernatural agencies first conceived of as independent were later hierarchized, to be finally synthesized in the idea of God.[3] Similarly, in the so-called 'metaphysical state',

---

3. These three secondary phases are designated by Comte as 'fetishism', 'polytheism', and 'monotheism'. It should hardly need saying that, quite to the contrary, it is 'monotheism', that is, the affirmation of the One Principle, that is necessarily the original stage; and indeed, in reality it is 'monotheism' alone that has always and everywhere existed, except for the incomprehension of the masses and in the extreme degeneration of certain traditional forms.

the notions of the different natural forces would have increasingly merged into that of a unique 'entity' called 'Nature';[4] moreover it can be seen from this that Comte was totally ignorant of what metaphysics actually is, for once it is a question of 'Nature' and of natural forces it is obviously a matter of 'physics', not 'metaphysics'; it would have been enough to refer to the etymology of the words in order to avoid such a misunderstanding. However that may be, we here see God and Nature considered no longer as two objects of knowledge, but merely as two notions to which the first two kinds of explanation envisaged in his hypothesis lead.[5] There remains Man, and although it is perhaps somewhat more difficult to see how he plays the same role with respect to the third 'explanation', he indeed does so in reality.

This results from the way in which Comte understands the various sciences. For him they have successively reached the 'positive state' in a certain order, each being prepared by those that precede it and without which it could not be established. Now the last of all the sciences according to this sequence, the one to which all the others lead and which thus represents the goal and summit of so-called 'positive' knowledge, a science that Comte made his 'mission' to establish, is that to which he gave the rather barbarous name of 'sociology', a term that has since passed into common usage; and this 'sociology' is properly the science of Man, or if preferred of Humanity, naturally envisaged from a 'social' point of view alone; besides, no other science of man is possible for Comte, for he believes that all that especially characterizes the human being and rightly belongs to him to the exclusion of other living beings, arises uniquely from his social life. It is therefore perfectly logical, regardless of what some have said, that he should end up where he in fact did: impelled by the more or less conscious need to discover a kind of parallel between the 'positive state' and the two other 'states' such

4. Comte supposes, moreover, that whenever 'Nature' is spoken of in this way, it must be to some degree 'personified', as it was in certain eighteenth-century philosophico-literary declamations.

5. It is quite obvious that it is in fact no more than a mere hypothesis, and indeed a very poorly founded one, that Comte thus 'dogmatically' asserts by abusively calling it a 'law'.

as he conceives them, he sees its culmination in what he calls the 'religion of Humanity'.[6] Thus we see here, as the 'ideal' terms of the three 'states', respectively God, Nature, and Humanity. We will not dwell further on this point, for this suffices to show that the all too famous 'law of the three estates' really derives from a distortion of a false application of the ternary *Deus, Homo, Natura*; and what is rather astonishing is that no one seems to have even noticed it.

6. 'Humanity' conceived as the collectivity of all men past, present, and future is for him a veritable 'personification', for in the pseudo-religious part of his work he calls it the 'Great Being', a kind of profane caricature of 'Universal Man'.

21

PROVIDENCE
WILL
DESTINY

TO COMPLETE WHAT WE HAVE SAID about the ternary *Deus, Homo, Natura*, we will speak briefly about another ternary which obviously corresponds to it term for term, that is, Providence, Will, and Destiny considered as the three powers that govern the manifested universe. Considerations about this ternary have been especially developed in modern times by Fabre d'Olivet [1767–1825][1] on the basis of data of Pythagorean origin; moreover, he also refers secondarily to the Chinese tradition and in a manner suggesting that

---

1. Particularly in his *L'histoire philosophique du Genre humain*; it is from the introduction to this work (first published under the title *De l'État social de l'Homme*), except where otherwise indicated, that the citations to follow are taken. [An English translation by Nayán Louise Redfield, *Hermeneutic Interpretation of the Origin of the Social State of Man and of the Destiny of the Adamic Race*, hereafter cited as *Hermeneutic Interpretation*, was published by G. P. Putnam's Sons, New York and London, in 1915.] — In the *Examens des Vers dorés de Pythagore* [*The Golden Verses of Pythagoras*, tr. Nayán Louise Redfield (New York and London: G. P. Putnam's Sons, 1917), hereafter cited as *Golden Verses*], which appeared earlier, one also finds reflections on the same subject, but less clearly expressed. D'Olivet seems sometimes to regard Destiny and Will simply as correlatives, with Providence dominating both, which is incompatible with the correspondence we are concerned with here. — Let us mention incidentally that it was on the application of these three universal powers to the social order that Saint-Yves d'Alveydre built his theory of 'synarchy'.

he recognized its equivalence with the Great Triad.[2] 'Man,' he writes, 'is neither animal nor pure intelligence. He is an intermediate being, situated half-way between matter and spirit, or Heaven and Earth, and forming the link between them'; one can clearly recognize here the position and role of the middle term of the Far-Eastern Triad.

That universal Man[3] is a power is averred by all the sacred codes of nations; it is felt by all the sages; it is even avowed by all true savants.... These two powers, between which he finds himself placed, are Destiny and Providence. Beneath him is Destiny, *nature necéssitée et naturée* ['natured nature', nature bound by necessity]; above him is Providence, *nature libre et naturante* ['naturing nature', nature in its freedom]. He is himself, as Kingdom of Man [*règne hominal*], the mediatory will, the efficient form, placed between these two natures to serve them as a link, a means of communication and to unite two actions, two movements, which would be incompatible without him.[4]

It is interesting to note that the two extreme terms of the ternary are expressly designated as *Natura naturans* and *Natura naturata*, in conformity with what we said above; and the two actions or the two movements in question are in the final analysis nothing but the action and reaction of Heaven and Earth, the alternating movement of *yang* and *yin*.

These three powers which I have just named—Providence, Man considered as the Kingdom of Man, and Destiny—constitute the universal ternary. Nothing escapes their action; all is subject to them in the universe; all except *God* Himself who, enveloping

---

2. He seems, moreover, to have hardly known anything but the Confucian side of it, although in *The Golden Verses of Pythagoras* he sometimes does cite Lao Tzu.

3. This expression must be understood here in a restricted sense, for the notion does not appear to extend beyond the properly human state. Indeed, it is evident that when this idea of 'universal Man' is transposed to include the totality of the states of the being, one can no longer speak of the 'Kingdom of Man', which really has no meaning except in our world.

4. *Hermeneutic Interpretation*, pp xxxviii–xl. ED.

them in His unfathomable Unity, forms with it the Sacred Tetrad of the ancients, that immense quaternary, which is All in All and outside of which there is nothing.[5]

This is an allusion to the fundamental quaternary of the Pythagoreans, symbolized by the *Tetraktys*, and what we said about it earlier in connection with the ternary *Spiritus, Anima, Corpus* enables us to understand things well enough that there is no reason to return to it. But it must also be noted—for this is particularly important from the point of view of concordances—that 'God' is envisaged here as the Principle in itself, in contrast to the first term in the ternary *Deus, Homo, Natura*, so that in these two cases the same word is not taken in the same sense; and here, Providence is only the instrument used by God in the government of the universe, in exactly the same way that Heaven is the instrument of the Principle in the Far-Eastern tradition.

Now, to understand why the middle term is identified here not only with man but more precisely with human Will, we should know that for Fabre d'Olivet the will is, in the human being, the inner and central element that unites and embraces[6] the intellectual, animic, and instinctive spheres, to which respectively correspond spirit, soul, and body. Moreover, since we must find in the 'microcosm' a correspondence with the 'macrocosm', these three spheres are analogous to the three universal powers which are Providence, Will, and Destiny;[7] and the will plays with respect to these a role that makes it a kind of image of the Principle itself. This way of envisaging the will (which, it must be said, is insufficiently justified by considerations of an order more psychological than truly metaphysical) must be related to our earlier remarks on the subject of alchemical Sulphur, for this is really what is in question. Furthermore, there is a kind of parallel between the three powers, for on the

5. *Hermeneutic Interpretation*, p xli. Ed.

6. It must be remarked here once again that it is the center that in reality contains all.

7. One will recall what we said in connection with the 'three worlds' about the more particular correspondence between Man and the animic or psychic domain.

one hand Providence can obviously be conceived as the expression of the Divine Will, and on the other Destiny is itself like a kind of obscure will of Nature.

Destiny is the inferior and instinctive part of Universal Nature[8] which I have called *nature naturée* ['natured nature']. Its own action is called *fatality*. The form by which it manifests itself to us is called *necessity.* . . . Providence is the superior and intelligent part of Universal Nature, which I have called *nature naturante* ['naturing nature']. It is a living law emanating from the Divinity, by means of which all things are determined in potentiality to be. . . .[9] It is the Will of Man [corresponding to the animic aspect of Universal Nature], which, as powerful medium, unites Destiny and Providence; without it, these two extreme powers not only would never unite, but they would not even understand each other.[10]

Another point also worthy of note is this: human will, by uniting with Providence and by consciously collaborating with it,[11] can balance Destiny and finally neutralize it.[12] Fabre d'Olivet says that

8. 'Nature' is here taken in the most general sense, and it thus includes, as 'three natures in one Nature', all three terms of the 'universal ternary', that is, in the final analysis, everything that is not the Principle itself.

9. This expression is inexact, since potentiality belongs on the contrary to the other pole of manifestation; one should say 'principially' or 'in essence'.

10. [*Hermeneutic Interpretation*, pp xlii–xliii]. Elsewhere, Fabre d'Olivet names as the respective agents of these three universal powers those beings which the Pythagoreans called the 'immortal Gods', the 'glorified Heroes', and the 'terrestrial Demons', 'relative to their respective elevation the harmonious position of the three worlds which they inhabit' (*Golden Verses*, Third Examination, p138).

11. To collaborate thus with Providence is what is referred to in Masonic terminology as working toward the realization of the 'plan of the Great Architect of the Universe' (cf. *Perspectives on Initiation*, chap. 31).

12. This is what was expressed by the Rosicrucians in the adage *Sapiens dominabitur astris* [the wise will rule the stars], the 'astral influences' representing, as we explained above, the totality of all the influences emanating from the cosmic environment and acting upon the individual to determine him outwardly.

the harmony between Will and Providence constitutes Good; Evil is born of their opposition....[13] Man is perfected or depraved, according as he tends to merge with the Universal Unity or to become distinguished from it;[14]

that is, according as he tends toward one or the other of the two poles of manifestation,[15] which in fact correspond to unity and multiplicity, and thus allies his will to Providence or to Destiny, and in this way turns either to the side of 'liberty', or to that of 'necessity'. He also writes that 'providential law is the law of the divine man, who principally lives the intellectual life, which is governed by that law'; however, he does not clarify what he means here by this 'divine man', who doubtless can be assimilated to 'transcendent man' or only to 'true man', as the case may be. According to Pythagorean doctrine, which was followed on this point as on so many others by Plato, 'Will exerted by faith [and thereby related to Providence] could subjugate Necessity itself, command Nature, and work miracles.' Equilibrium between Will and Providence on the one hand and Destiny on the other was symbolized geometrically by a right triangle with sides respectively proportional to the numbers 3, 4, and 5, a triangle to which Pythagorism attached great importance[16] and which, by a remarkable coincidence, plays no less important a role in the Far-Eastern tradition. If Providence is represented by 3, human Will by 4, and Destiny by 5, we have in this triangle $3^2 + 4^2 =$

---

13. Fundamentally this equates good and evil with the two contrary tendencies we are about to mention, together with all their consequences.

14. *Golden Verses*, Twelfth Examination, p169. ED.

15. These are the two opposing tendencies, one ascending and the other descending, which in the Hindu tradition are termed *sattva* and *tamas*.

16. This triangle is found in Masonic symbolism, and we alluded to it in connection with the Worshipful Master's square; the complete triangle itself appears in the insignia of the Past Master. Let us take this occasion to say that a considerable portion of Masonic symbolism derives directly from Pythagorism through an unbroken 'chain' including the Roman *Collegia Fabrorum* and the medieval builders' guilds. The triangle in question here is an example of this direct transmission, and the Blazing Star, identical to the *Pentalpha* which served as a 'means of recognition' for the Pythagoreans, is another (cf. *Perspectives on Initiation*, chap. 16).

5^2;[17] raising the numbers to the second power indicates that this relates to the domain of universal forces, that is, the animic domain,[18] corresponding to Man in the 'macrocosm', and at whose center, as middle term, lies the Will in the 'microcosm'.[19]

17. Here again we find 3 as a 'celestial' number and 5 as a 'terrestrial' number, as in the Far-Eastern tradition, although here they are not envisaged as correlative, since 3 is there associated with 2, and 5 with 6, as we explained earlier; as for the number 4, it corresponds to the cross as symbol of 'Universal Man'.

18. This domain is actually the second of the 'three worlds', whether one envisages them in an ascending or a descending order; the raising to successive powers, representing degrees of increasing universalization, corresponds to the ascending direction (cf. *The Symbolism of the Cross*, chap. 12 and *The Metaphysical Principles of the Infinitesimal Calculus*, chap. 20).

19. According to Fabre d'Olivet's schematization, this center of the animic sphere is also the tangential point of the two other spheres, the intellectual and the instinctive, the centers of which are located at diametrically opposite points on the circumference of that same median sphere:

> By projecting its circumference, this center reaches the other centers and joins to itself the opposite points of the two circumferences projected by those centers [i.e., the lowest point of the one circumference and the highest point of the other]. In this way the three vital spheres move within each other and so communicate their own natures to each other, transferring their reciprocal influences from one sphere to another.

The circumferences representing two consecutive spheres (intellectual and animic, animic and instinctive) therefore present the arrangement whose properties we noted in connection with figure 3, each passing through the center of the other.

22

TRIPLE TIME

NOTWITHSTANDING all we have just said, one can still ask the question, is there in the order of spatial and temporal determinations something that corresponds to the three terms of the Great Triad and the equivalent ternaries? As concerns space, there is no difficulty in finding such a correspondence, for it is immediately given by consideration of the 'above' and 'below', envisaged, according to the usual geometrical representation, with respect to a horizontal plane taken as 'level of reference', which for us is naturally that which corresponds to the domain of the human state itself. This plane may be regarded as median, first from the fact that it appears to us as such because of our own 'perspective', insofar as it is that of the state in which we presently find ourselves, and also because we can at least virtually locate on it the center of all states of manifestation. For these reasons it clearly corresponds to Man as the middle term of the Triad, as well as to man understood in the ordinary and individual sense. Relative to that plane, what is above represents the 'celestial' aspects of the Cosmos and what is below represents its 'terrestrial' aspects, the respective extreme limits of the two regions into which space is thus divided (limits which are indefinitely removed in both directions) being the two poles of manifestation, that is, Heaven and Earth themselves, which from the plane in question are seen through those relatively 'celestial' and 'terrestrial' aspects. The corresponding influences are expressed by two contrary tendencies which can be related to the two halves of the vertical axis, the upper half acting in an ascending direction, the lower in a descending direction, starting from the median plane. As this naturally corresponds to expansion in a horizontal direction intermediate between the two opposing tendencies, we also see here the correspondence of the three *gunas* of Hindu tradition with the three terms of the Triad:[1] *sattva* thus corresponds to Heaven, *rajas* to Man, and *tamas* to Earth.[2] If the median plane is regarded as the diametral plane of a sphere (which must, moreover, be considered of indefinite radius since it contains the totality of space), the upper and lower hemispheres are, according to another symbolism we have mentioned, the two halves of the 'World Egg', which, after their separation as a result of the effective determination of the median plane, respectively become Heaven and Earth, understood here in their most general meaning;[3] in the center of the median plane is *Hiranyagarbha*, which appears thus in the Cosmos as the 'eternal *Avatāra*' and is thereby identical with 'Universal Man'.[4]

As for time, the matter would seem more difficult to resolve; nevertheless, here too we have a ternary since we speak of 'triple time' (*trikāla* in Sanskrit), that is, time envisaged under three modalities, which are the past, the present, and the future; but can these three modalities be related to the three terms of ternaries like those we are examining here? It must be said first of all that the present can be represented as a point dividing into two the line along which time unfolds, and thereby determining at each instant the separation (but also the juncture) between the past and the future of which it is the common boundary, just as the median plane of which we were speaking above is the common boundary between the upper and lower hemispheres of space. As we have explained elsewhere,[5] the 'rectilinear' representation of time is both insufficient and inexact since time is really cyclical and since this characteristic is found even in its smallest subdivisions; but here we do not have to specify the form of the line in question, since whatever that form may be, for

1. Cf. *The Symbolism of the Cross*, chap. 5.
2. The reader will recall what we said above on the subject of the 'sattvic' or 'tamasic' character taken on by human will, in itself neutral or 'rajasic', depending on whether it allies itself to Providence or to Destiny.
3. This should be related to our previous remarks on the two hemispheres in connection with the double spiral, as well as on the division of the *yin-yang* symbol into its two halves.
4. See *Perspectives on Initiation*, chap. 48.
5. *The Reign of Quantity and the Signs of the Times*, chap. 5.

the being situated at a point on that line the two parts into which it is divided will always appear to be respectively 'before' or 'after' that point, just as the two halves of space will appear to be 'above' and 'below', that is to say above and below the plane which is being taken as the 'level of reference'. To complete the parallel between spatial and temporal determinations, the point representing the present can always be taken in a certain sense as the 'middle of time', since from this point time can only appear to extend equally indefinitely in the two opposite directions that correspond to past and future. What is more, 'true man' occupies the center of the human state, that is, a point that must be truly 'central' with respect to all the conditions of that state, including the temporal condition;[6] one can say therefore that he is effectively situated at the 'middle of time', which he himself moreover determines by the fact that he dominates as it were the individual conditions,[7] just as in the Chinese tradition, by placing himself at the central point of the *Ming T'ang*, the Emperor determines the midpoint of the annual cycle. Thus the 'middle of time' is strictly, if one may so put it, the temporal 'place' of 'true man', and for him this point is always the present.

If, then, the present closely corresponds to Man (and even for the ordinary human being it is obviously only in the present that he can exercise his action, at least in a direct and immediate way)[8] it remains to be seen whether there is not also a certain correspondence between the past and future and the two other terms of the Triad, and here again it is a comparison between the spatial and temporal determinations that will provide the clue. The states of manifestation that are relatively speaking inferior and superior with respect to the human state, and which are depicted in spatial symbolism as located above or below it, are on the other hand described

6. There is no reason to speak here of 'transcendent man', for he is entirely beyond the temporal condition as well as all others; but if he happens to situate himself in the human state as we described earlier, he will occupy therein *a fortiori* the central position in all respects.

7. Cf. *Perspectives on Initiation*, chap. 42 and also *The Esoterism of Dante*, chap. 8.

8. If 'true man' can exercise an influence at any given moment in time, this is because, from the central point which he occupies, he can at will render that moment present for himself.

according to a temporal symbolism as constituting cycles respectively anterior and posterior to the present cycle. The totality of these states thus forms two domains whose action, insofar as it makes itself felt in the human state, is expressed by influences that can be called 'terrestrial' on the one hand and 'celestial' on the other, in the sense we have consistently given these terms here, and appears therein as the respective manifestations of Destiny and of Providence, a fact the Hindu tradition indicates very clearly in attributing the first of these two domains to the *Asuras* and the other to the *Devas*. In fact, perhaps it is by envisaging the two extreme terms of the Triad under the aspects of Destiny and Providence that the correspondence is most clearly visible; and this is precisely why the past appears as 'necessary' and the future as 'free', which is exactly the characteristic of these two powers. It is quite true that all this is really just a question of 'perspective', and that for a being outside of the temporal condition there is no longer a past or a future, nor consequently any difference between them, everything appearing to it in perfect simultaneity;[9] but here we are of course speaking from the point of view of a being which, since it exists in time, is necessarily placed between past and future. Destiny, says Fabre d'Olivet on this subject,

gives the principle of nothing but takes possession of it as soon as it is given in order to dominate the consequences. It is by the necessity of those consequences alone that it influences the future and makes itself felt in the present; for all that it possesses personally is in the past. Thus by Destiny we understand that power by which we conceive that the things created are created, that they are thus and not otherwise, and that once placed according to their nature they have forced results which are developed successively and necessarily.[10]

9. This is all the more so for the Principle itself. It is worth noting in this connection that the Hebrew Tetragrammaton is considered to be formed grammatically by the contraction of the three tenses of the verb 'to be'. It thereby designates the Principle, that is, pure Being, which contains within itself the three terms of the 'universal ternary' (as Fabre d'Olivet calls it), just as Eternity, which is inherent in it, envelops within itself 'triple time'.

10. *Hermeneutic Interpretation*, p xlii. Ed.

It must be said that he is much less clear about the temporal correspondence of the other two powers, and that, in a work written earlier than the one we just cited,[11] he even reverses it in a way that seems hard to explain:[12]

> The Will of man, in exercising its activity, modifies coexistent [and therefore present] things, creates from them new ones which immediately become the property of Destiny, and prepares for the future changes in what was made, and necessary consequences for what has just been done....[13] The aim of Providence is to bring all beings to perfection, and of this perfection it receives the irrefragable model from God Himself. The means that it has to attain this end is what we call time. But time does not exist for it according to our ideas;[14] it conceives it as a movement in eternity.[15]

All of this is not perfectly clear, but what is missing can easily be supplied; moreover, we have just done this as concerns Man, and so

11. We have been unable to trace this earlier source, but the passage concerned is virtually identical with one following closely on (Ibid., pxliii) that cited in the preceding note. ED.

12. In his *The Golden Verses of Pythagoras* (Twelfth Examination) he says that 'the power of Will was exercised upon the things to be done, or upon the future; the necessity of Destiny, upon the things done, or upon the past.... [Thus] liberty rules in the future, necessity in the past, and Providence over the present' [*Golden Verses*, pp167–68]. This is equivalent to making Providence the median term and, by making 'freedom' the proper characteristic of Will, making it the opposite of Destiny, which does not agree at all with the real relationships of these three terms as he himself explains them a little later.

13. It can be said that the Will works with a view to the future inasmuch as it is a continuation of the present, but this of course is not at all the same as saying that it acts directly upon the future itself as such.

14. This should be obvious, since Providence corresponds to what is superior to the human state, of which time is only one of the special conditions; but it is worth adding for more precision that it makes use of time inasmuch as, for us, it moves 'forward', that is, in the direction of the future, which implies moreover that the past belongs to Destiny.

15. This seems to be an allusion to what the Scholastics called *aevum* or *aeviternitas*, terms that designate modes of duration other than time that condition 'angelic' states, that is, supra-individual states, and which do indeed appear to be 'celestial' with respect to the human state.

also as concerns Will. As for Providence, from the traditional point of view it is a current notion that, according to the Koranic expression, 'God holds the keys of hidden things,'[16] thus, in particular, those that, in our world, are not yet manifested;[17] for the future is indeed hidden for men, at least under usual conditions. Now it is obvious that a being, whatever it may be, can have no hold over what it does not know, and consequently that man cannot act directly upon the future, which from his temporal 'perspective' is merely what does not yet exist. Indeed, this idea has persisted even in the popular mentality, which, perhaps without a very clear understanding of what it is saying, expresses it by proverbs such as 'man proposes, God disposes', that is to say that although man may strive in the measure of his ability to prepare for the future, this will never be anything but what God wants it to be, or what he will make it to be by the action of his Providence (from which it results moreover that the Will will act more efficaciously in view of the future as it is more closely united with Providence); and it is also said, even more explicitly, that 'the present belongs to men but the future belongs to God'. On this score, then, there can be no doubt, and of the three modalities of 'triple time' it is indeed the future that is the proper domain of Providence, as is required moreover by its symmetry with Destiny, whose proper domain is the past, for this symmetry must necessarily result from the fact that these two powers represent respectively the two extreme terms of the 'universal ternary'.

16. Koran 6:59.

17. We say 'in particular' because it goes without saying that in reality these are only an infinitesimal part of the 'hidden things' (*al-ghayb*) that together make up the unmanifested.

23

THE COSMIC WHEEL

IN CERTAIN WORKS linked to the Hermetic tradition[1] we find references to the ternary *Deus, Homo, Rota*, that is to say that in the third term we examined earlier, *Natura* has been replaced by *Rota*, or the 'Wheel'. This is the 'cosmic wheel' which, as we have already said on different occasions, is a symbol of the manifested world, which the Rosicrucians called *Rota Mundi*, the 'wheel of the world'.[2] It can therefore be said that, in general, this symbol represents Nature taken, as we have said, in its widest sense; but it is also susceptible of various other, more precise, meanings, among which we shall consider here only those directly relating to the subject of our study.

The geometrical figure from which the wheel is derived is the circle with its center; in its most universal sense, the center represents the Principle, symbolized geometrically by the point as it is arithmetically by unity, and the circumference represents manifestation, which is 'measured' by the radius emanating from the Principle;[3] but this figure, so simple in appearance, nevertheless has a multiplicity of applications corresponding to various more or less particularized points of view.[4] For example, and this is especially relevant

---

1. Especially in the *Absconditorum Clavis* ['The Key of Hidden Things'] of Guillaume Postel. — It may be noted that the title of this work is the literal equivalent of the Koranic passage cited a bit earlier.

2. Cf. the figure of the *Rota Mundi* presented by Leibnitz in his treatise *De arte combinatoria* (see the foreword to *The Metaphysical Principles of the Infinitesimal Calculus*); like the *Dharma-chakra*, of which we shall speak shortly, this figure is a wheel of eight spokes.

3. Cf. *The Reign of Quantity and the Signs of the Times*, chap. 3.

4. In astrology, this is the sign for the sun, which is for us in fact the center of the sensible world, and which for that very reason is traditionally taken as a symbol

here, since the Principle acts in the Cosmos by means of Heaven, Heaven too can be represented by the center, and the circumference, where its rays in fact terminate, will then represent the other pole of manifestation, that is to say Earth, and the corresponding circle will in this case represent the entire cosmic domain. Furthermore, the center represents unity and the circumference multiplicity, which expresses quite well the respective characteristics of universal Essence and Substance. One could also limit oneself to the consideration of a determinate world or state of existence alone; in that case the center will naturally be the point where the 'Activity of Heaven' manifests itself in that state, and the circumference will represent the *materia secunda* of that world, which, relative to this, plays a role corresponding to that of *materia prima* in regard to the totality of universal manifestation.[5]

The figure of the wheel differs from the one we have just spoken of only by the inclusion of a number of radii, which more explicitly mark the relationship between the circumference at which they terminate and the center from which they originate; and it goes without saying that the circumference cannot exist without its center, while the latter is absolutely independent of the former and contains principially all possible concentric circumferences, which are determined by the greater or lesser length of the radii. These radii can of course be depicted by any number of lines, since they are really indefinitely many like the points on the circumference which are their extremities; but in fact the traditional representations always consist of numbers having a particular symbolic value that, together with the general significance of the wheel, defines its particular

---

of the 'Heart of the World' (cf. *Perspectives on Initiation*, chap. 47); we have said enough about the symbolism of the 'solar rays' that it should be hardly necessary to recall it here. In alchemy, this is the sign of gold, which as 'mineral light' corresponds among metals to the sun among the planets. In the science of numbers, it is the symbol of the denary insofar as this constitutes a complete numerical cycle; from this point of view, the center is 1 and the circumference 9, totaling together 10, for unity, being the very principle of numbers, must be placed at the center and not on the circumference, whose natural measure, moreover, is not accomplished by decimal division, as we explained above, but by division by the multiples of 3, 9, and 12.

5. More on this subject will be found in *The Reign of Quantity and the Signs of the Times*.

application according to the case.[6] The simplest form has just four radii dividing the circumference into equal parts, that is, two diameters at right angles forming a cross within the circumference.[7] From the spatial point of view this figure naturally corresponds to the four cardinal points;[8] from the temporal point of view, on the other hand, if the circumference is taken to be traversed in a certain direction, it becomes the image of a cycle of manifestation, and the divisions marked on it by the extremities of the arms of the cross then correspond to the different periods or phases into which the cycle is divided. Such a division can naturally be envisaged so to speak on different levels depending on the extent of the cycle in question.[9] Moreover, the idea of the wheel immediately evokes that of 'rotation', and this rotation symbolizes the continual change to which manifested things are subject, whence the expression 'wheel of becoming';[10] in this movement there is only a single point that remains fixed and unmoved, and this point is the center.[11]

There is no need here to further emphasize these notions; we will merely add that, if the center is first a beginning, it is also a point of completion: all things issue from it, and all must finally return to it. Since all things exist only by the Principle (or by what represents it relative to manifestation or to a certain state of manifestation), there must be a permanent link between them and it, represented by the

6. The forms most often met with are the wheels of six or eight spokes, as well as twelve and sixteen, which double them.

7. We have spoken elsewhere of the relationship between this symbol and the swastika (see The Symbolism of the Cross, chap. 10).

8. See above, figures 13 and 14.

9. Thus there are, for example, in the terrestrial order of existence alone, the four principal times of the day, the four phases of the lunar cycle, the four seasons of the year, and also, from another point of view, the four traditional ages of humanity as well as those of the individual human being; in short, all the quaternary correspondences of the kind already alluded to earlier.

10. Cf. the 'Wheel of Fortune' in Western antiquity, and the symbolism of the tenth arcana of the Tarot.

11. The center must also be conceived as principially containing the entire wheel, and that is why Guillaume Postel describes the center of Eden (which is itself both the 'center of the world' and its image) as 'the Wheel in the midst of the Wheel', which corresponds to what we said about the Ming T'ang.

radii that join all the points on the circumference to the center; but these radii can be traversed in two opposite directions: first from the center to the circumference, and then in return from the circumference to the center.[12] There are thus two complementary phases, the first of which is represented by a centrifugal movement and the second by a centripetal movement;[13] it is these phases that are traditionally compared to those of respiration, as well as to the double movement of the heart, as we have often pointed out. It will be seen that we have here a ternary consisting of center, radius and circumference, in which the radius plays precisely the role of the median term as we previously defined it; this is why, in the Far-Eastern Great Triad, Man is sometimes likened to a spoke of the 'cosmic wheel', whose center and circumference then correspond respectively to Heaven and Earth. As the radius emanating from the center 'measures' the cosmos or the domain of manifestation, so 'true man' will be seen to be the 'measure of all things' in this world, as likewise 'Universal Man' is for manifestation in its integrality;[14] and it is also worth noting that in the figure just spoken of, the cross formed by two right-angled diameters, which in a way are equivalent to all the radii of the circumference (for all the moments of a cycle are as it were summed up in its principal phases), is precisely, in its complete form, the very symbol of 'Universal Man'.[15]

Naturally, this symbolism is different, at least in appearance, from the one showing man at the very center of a state of existence and

12. One could therefore understand the reaction of the passive principle as a 'resistance' which checks the influences emanating from the active principle and limits their field of action; and this is also what the symbolism of the 'plane of reflection' indicates.

13. It must be carefully noted that, here, these two movements are considered in relation to the Principle and not in relation to manifestation; this is in order to avoid errors to which the neglect of 'inverse analogy' can lead.

14. See *The Symbolism of the Cross*, chap. 16.

15. For an interpretation of this same figure based on the numerical equivalents of its elements, see also Louis-Claude de Saint-Martin's *Tableau naturel des rapports qui existent entre Dieu, l'Homme et l'Univers*, chapter 18. — The title of this work is often abbreviated as *Tableau naturel*, but we give its full title here to show that because the word 'Universe' is taken here in the sense of 'Nature' in general, it contains an explicit mention of the ternary *Deus, Homo, Natura*.

'Universal Man' as identified with the 'World Axis', because it corresponds to a point of view which is also different to a certain extent;
but fundamentally they are nonetheless in perfect agreement as to
their essential meaning, and one need only be careful, as always in
such a case, not to confuse the various meanings which might be
attributed to their constituent elements.[16] It is worth observing that
at every point on the circumference, and relative to that point, the
direction of the tangent can be regarded as horizontal, and consequently the radius perpendicular to it can be regarded as vertical, so
that every radius is in a sense a virtual axis. 'Above' and 'below' can
accordingly be regarded as the two opposing directions along the
radius; but whereas in the order of sensible appearances 'below' is
toward the center (in this case the center of the earth),[17] here it is
necessary to apply 'inverse analogy' and view the center as in reality
the highest point;[18] and thus, from whatever point on the circumference one starts, the highest point will always remain the same.
Man, assimilated to the spoke of the wheel, must then be represented with his feet on the circumference of the wheel and his head
touching the center; and indeed, one can say that in the 'microcosm',
in every respect, the feet correspond to Earth and the head to
Heaven.[19]

16. To give another example related to the same subject, in the Hindu tradition,
and sometimes also in the Far-Eastern tradition, Heaven and Earth are represented
as the two wheels of the 'cosmic chariot'; the 'World Axis' is then represented by the
axle which joins the two wheels at their centers, and which for that reason must be
thought of as vertical, like the 'bridge' we spoke of earlier. In this case, the correspondence of the different parts of the chariot is obviously not the same as when, as
we said above, it is the canopy and the floor which respectively represent Heaven
and Earth, and where the chariot-pole is then the symbol of the 'World Axis'
(which corresponds to the position of an ordinary chariot). Moreover, the wheels
here are not taken especially into consideration.

17. Cf. The Esoterism of Dante, chap. 8.

18. This 'reversal' results from the fact that, in the first case, man is placed outside the circumference (which then represents the terrestrial surface), while in the
second he is inside it.

19. It was to yet further emphasize this correspondence, already evident from
the very form of the feet and head as well as from their respective positions, that the
early Confucians wore round caps and square shoes, which is also connected with
our earlier remarks about the ritual garments of princes.

24

THE *TRIRATNA*

IN BRINGING TO A CLOSE our examination of the concordances
among the different traditional ternaries, we will say a few words
here about the ternary of *Buddha, Dharma, Sangha*, which latter
together make up the *Triratna* or 'triple jewel', and which certain
Western writers have improperly referred to as a 'Buddhist Trinity'.
It must be said at the outset that it is not possible to make its terms
correspond exactly and completely to the terms of the Great Triad;
nevertheless, such a correspondence may be envisaged at least in
certain respects. First of all, to begin with what is clearest in this
connection, the *Sangha* or 'Assembly',[1] that is to say the Buddhist
community, obviously represents the properly human element;
from the special point of view of Buddhism, it takes the place of
Humanity itself[2] because it is its 'central' portion, that with respect
to which all the rest is envisaged,[3] and also because, in a general
way, every particular traditional form can only occupy itself directly
with its actual adherents, and not with those who are, so to speak,
outside of its 'jurisdiction'. Moreover, the 'central' position ascribed
to the *Sangha* within the human order is really justified (as its
equivalents in every other tradition would also be, for the same

---

1. We avoid the use of the term 'Church', which, although it has approximately
the same meaning etymologically, has taken on a special meaning in Christianity
which cannot be applied elsewhere, just as the word 'Synagogue', which has even
more exactly the same original meaning, has for its part acquired a specifically Jew-
ish sense.

2. Here it may be remembered what we said in the beginning about the similar
role of the term *huei*, or of what it represents, in the case of the *T'ien Ti Huei*.

3. We have already explained this point of view in another case, apropos of the
'central' position ascribed to the Chinese Empire.

reason) by the presence in its midst of *Arhats* who have attained the degree of 'true man'[4] and consequently are effectively situated at the very center of the human state.

As for the Buddha, he can be said to represent the transcendent element through which the influence of Heaven is manifested, and who consequently 'incarnates' so to speak this influence with respect to his direct or indirect disciples who transmit participation in it to each other in a continual 'chain', by means of the rites of admission into the *Sangha*. In saying this of the Buddha we are thinking less of the historical personage in himself, whatever he may have been in fact (which has only a very secondary importance from the point of view we take here) than that which he represents[5] in virtue of the symbolic characteristics attributed to him,[6] by which he appears above all in the character of an *Avatāra*.[7] The manifestation of the Buddha is, in sum, the 'redescent from Heaven to Earth' spoken of by the Emerald Tablet, and the being who thus brings celestial influences into the world after having 'incorporated' them into his own

4. The *Bodhisattvas*, who can be considered to correspond to the degree of 'transcendent man', escape by that very fact from the terrestrial community and reside in the 'Heavens', from whence they 'return' by way of a 'descending' realization only in order to manifest themselves as Buddhas.

5. Moreover, it is only in this regard that the name Buddha is given to him and truly belongs to him, since it is not the proper name of an individual, which moreover could not be truly applied in such a case (cf. *Perspectives on Initiation*, chap. 27).

6. To say that these characteristics are symbolic does not in any way mean that they were not in fact possessed by a real personage (and we will even say quite readily that they are all the more real to the extent that his individuality is effaced before these characteristics); we have spoken frequently enough about the symbolic value necessarily possessed by historical facts themselves that there is no need to stress the point further (cf. *The Symbolism of the Cross*), and we will merely take this opportunity to repeat once again that 'historical truth only possesses substance when it derives from the Principle' (*Chuang Tzu*, chap. 25).

7. For a more detailed treatment of this subject we can do no better than refer the reader to the various works in which Ananda K. Coomaraswamy has discussed the question, especially his *Elements of Buddhist Iconography* (New Delhi: Munshiram Manoharlal, 1979) [first edition 1935], and 'The Nature of Buddhist Art' [reprinted in *Coomaraswamy 1: Selected Papers, Traditional Art and Symbolism* ed. Roger Lipsey (Princeton: Bollingen Series, Princeton University Press, 1977)].

nature can truly be said to represent Heaven with regard to the human domain. Assuredly this conception is far removed from the 'rationalized' Buddhism with which Westerners have been familiarized by the work of orientalists; it may correspond to a 'Mahāyānist' point of view, but that for us cannot be a valid objection, for it indeed seems that the 'Hīnayānist' point of view, which is commonly presented as 'original' (doubtless because it agrees only too well with certain preconceived ideas), may on the contrary be no more than the product of a mere degeneration.

Moreover, the correlation just mentioned must not be taken as an identification pure and simple, for if in a certain sense the Buddha represents the 'celestial' principle, he does so only in a relative sense insofar as he is really the 'mediator', that is, insofar as he plays the role which is properly that of 'Universal Man'.[8] Thus as regards the *Sangha*, we were obliged, in order to assimilate it to Humanity, to restrict ourselves to the consideration of this in the exclusively individual sense (including the state of 'true man', who is still but the perfection of the individuality); and it must be added that Humanity here seems to be conceived 'collectively' (since it is a matter of the 'Assembly') rather than 'specifically'. It can thus be said that, if we have found here a relationship comparable to that between Heaven and Man, the two terms of this relationship are nevertheless included in what the Far-Eastern tradition designates as 'Man' in the most complete and 'comprehensive' sense of this word, and which must contain in itself an image of the Great Triad in its entirety.

As to the *Dharma* or 'Law', it is more difficult to find a precise correspondence, even with the reservations we just formulated for the two other terms of the ternary; besides, the word *dharma* in Sanskrit has multiple meanings which one must know how to distinguish in the different cases where it is used, and which make a general definition almost impossible. Nevertheless, it can be said that the root of this word has the meaning of 'to support',[9] and in this way makes a

8. See our earlier discussion of 'transcendent man' and 'true man', and of the relationships between the different grades of the Taoist and Confucian hierarchies.

9. The root *dhri* means to 'carry', 'support', 'hold up', 'maintain'.

connection with the Earth that 'supports', as we explained above; in sum it is a question of a principle of the conservation of beings, thus of stability, at least insofar as this is compatible with the conditions of manifestation, for *dharma* in all its applications is always concerned with the manifested world; and, as we said earlier in connection with the role ascribed to Niu Kua, the function of assuring the stability of the world is associated with the 'substantial' side of manifestation. It is true, on the other hand, that the idea of stability refers to something which in the domain of change itself escapes change and thus must be situated in the 'Invariable Middle'; but this is something that comes from the 'substantial' pole, that is, from the side of terrestrial influences, by way of the lower part of the axis traversed in the ascending direction.[10] Moreover, the notion of *dharma* so understood is not limited to man but extends to all beings and to all their states of manifestation; it can thus be said that in itself it belongs to the cosmic order; but in the Buddhist idea of the 'Law' it is applied specifically to the human order, so that if it has a certain relative correspondence with the lowest term of the Great Triad, it is still in relation to Humanity, always in the individual sense, that the term must be envisaged here.

It can also be said that in the idea of 'law', in all the senses and with all the applications of which it is susceptible, there is always a certain character of 'necessity'[11] or 'constraint' which puts it on the side of 'Destiny', and also that, for every manifested being, *dharma* in the final analysis expresses conformity to the conditions imposed on it from outside by environment, that is, by 'Nature' in the most extended sense of this word. One can therefore understand why the principal symbol of the Buddhist *Dharma* is the wheel, according to

---

10. The root *dhri* is also related both in form and in meaning to another root, *dhru*, from which is derived *dhruva*, designating the pole; thus we can say that the idea of 'pole' or 'axis' of the manifested world plays an important role in the idea of *dharma* itself. — Regarding stability or immobility as an inverted reflection of principial immutability at the very lowest point of manifestation, cf. *The Reign of Quantity and the Signs of the Times*, chap. 20.

11. According to the case, this necessity can be logical or mathematical, 'physical', or even that called, rather improperly moreover, 'moral'; the Buddhist *Dharma* naturally falls into this last category.

our earlier explanation of this;[12] and at the same time this figure allows one to see that it is a passive principle that is passive in relation to the Buddha, since it is he who 'turns the wheel of the Law'.[13] Moreover, this is necessarily so, since the Buddha is on the side of celestial influences as the *Dharma* is on the side of terrestrial influences; and we might add that by the very fact that he is beyond the conditions of the manifested world, the Buddha would have nothing in common with the *Dharma*[14] if he did not have to apply it to Humanity, just as, according to what was said earlier, Providence would have nothing in common with Destiny were it not for Man, who links these two extreme terms of the 'universal ternary' together.

12. The *Dharma-chakra*, or 'wheel of the Law', is generally a wheel of eight spokes; these, which in spatial symbolism can naturally be compared to the four cardinal and four intermediary points, correspond in Buddhism itself to the eight paths of the 'Excellent Way' as well as to the eight petals of the 'Lotus of the True Law' (which can also be compared with the eight 'beatitudes' of the Gospels). A similar arrangement is found, moreover, in the eight *kua* or trigrams of Fu Hsi, and in this connection it is worth noting that the title of the *I Ching* is itself interpreted as meaning the 'book of mutations' or 'of changes in the turning of the circle', a meaning which is obviously related to the symbolism of the wheel.

13. He plays therefore a similar role to *Chakravartī* or the 'universal monarch', in another application of the symbolism of the wheel; it is also said that Shakyamuni had to choose between the function of Buddha and that of *Chakravartī*.

14. This absence of any connection with *Dharma* corresponds to the state of *Pratyeka-Buddha*, who, having attained the goal of total realization, does not 're-descend' into manifestation.

25

THE CITY
OF WILLOWS

ALTHOUGH WE STATED at the beginning of this book that we had
no intention of analyzing the symbolism found in the rituals of the
T'ien Ti Huei, there is nonetheless one point to which we wish to
draw attention, because it clearly refers to a 'polar' symbolism not
unconnected with some of our present considerations. Whatever the
particular forms it may assume, the 'primordial' character of such a
symbolism is particularly clear from what we have said about orientation; and this is easy to understand since the center is the 'place'
which properly corresponds to the 'primordial state', and also since
the center and the pole are at root one and the same thing, for both
are the unique point that remains fixed and invariable throughout
all the revolutions of the 'wheel of becoming'.[1] The center of the
human state can therefore be represented as the terrestrial pole, and
that of the total Universe as the celestial pole; and one can say that
the first is thus the 'place' of 'true man', and the second that of 'transcendent man'. Moreover, the terrestrial pole is as the reflection of
the celestial pole because, insofar as it is identified with the center, it
is the point where the 'Activity of Heaven' directly manifests itself;
and these two poles are joined by the 'World Axis', along which the
'Activity of Heaven' is exercised.[2] This is why certain stellar symbols,

---

1. For a more detailed treatment of polar symbolism we refer the reader to our
study *The King of the World*.
2. These are the two extremities of the axle of the 'cosmic chariot' when its two
wheels are taken to represent Heaven and Earth, according to the meaning of these
two terms in the *Tribhuvana*.

which properly belong to the celestial pole, can also be related to the terrestrial pole, where they are reflected, if one may so express oneself, by 'projection' in the corresponding domain. From that point, except for cases where these two poles are expressly marked by distinct symbols, there is no reason to distinguish them, for the same symbolism applies at two different degrees of universality; and this, which implies the virtual identity of the center of the human state with that of the total being,[3] also agrees with what we have said above, that from the human point of view, 'true man' cannot be distinguished from the 'trace' of 'transcendent man'.

In the initiation into the *T'ien Ti Huei*, the neophyte, after having passed through a number of preliminary stages, the last of which is called the 'Circle of Heaven and Earth' (*T'ien Ti Ch'üan*), finally arrives at the 'City of Willows' (*Mu Yang Ch'eng*), which is also called the 'House of the Great Peace' (*T'ai P'ing Chuang*).[4] The first of these two names is explained by the fact that in China the willow is a symbol of immortality; it is therefore equivalent to the acacia in Freemasonry or to the 'golden bough' in the ancient mysteries;[5] and because of this meaning the 'City of Willows' is properly the 'Abode of the Immortals'.[6] As to the second of these names, it also indicates as clearly as possible that it refers to a place considered to be 'central',[7] for the 'Great Peace' (*as-Sakīnah* in Arabic)[8] is the same thing as the *Shekinah* of the Hebrew Kabbalah, that is, as the 'divine presence' which is the very manifestation of the 'Activity of Heaven'

---

3. See our treatment of this subject in *The Symbolism of the Cross*.

4. See B. Favre, *Les Sociétés secrètes en Chine*, chap. 8. — Although the author has correctly understood the significance of the symbolism of the dipper, to which we shall shortly come, he has been unable to draw out its most important consequences.

5. See *The Esoterism of Dante*, chap. 5.

6. On the 'abode of immortality', cf. *The King of the World*, chap 7, and *The Reign of Quantity and the Signs of the Times*, chap. 23.

7. In Masonic symbolism the acacia is similarly located in the 'Middle Chamber'.

8. See *The King of the World*, chap. 3 and *The Symbolism of the Cross*, chaps. 7 and 8. — This is also the *Pax profunda* of the Rosicrucians; and it may be recalled that in the nineteenth century the title 'Great Peace' (*T'ai P'ing*) was adopted by an organization arising from the *Pai Lien Huei* [see Preface to this volume].

and which, as we said earlier, can only reside in such a place or in a traditional 'sanctuary' assimilated to it. In accordance with what we have just said, moreover, this center can represent either the center of the human world or that of the Universe as a whole; the fact that it is beyond the 'Circle of Heaven and Earth' expresses, according to the first meaning, that he who reaches it escapes by that very fact from the movement of the 'cosmic wheel' and from the vicissitudes of *yin* and *yang*, and thus from alternation of lives and deaths which is their consequence, so that he can be truly termed 'immortal';[9] and, according to the second, there is a rather explicit allusion to the 'extra-cosmic' location of the 'pinnacle of Heaven'.

What is also quite remarkable is that the 'City of Willows' is ritually represented by a dipping bowl filled with rice in which are planted a number of symbolic standards;[10] this figure may seem rather strange, but it is easily explained by the fact that the 'Dipper' (*Tou*) is in China the name given to the Great Bear.[11] Now, the importance traditionally given to this constellation is well known, and in the Hindu tradition especially the Great Bear (*saptariksha*) is

9. For 'true man' this is still only a virtual immortality, but it will become fully effective by direct passage from the human state to the supreme and unconditioned state (cf. *Man and His Becoming according to the Vedānta*, chap. 18).

10. Here a connection can be made with the standards in the 'Camp of the Princes' in the 'chart' used by the 32nd grade of Scottish Freemasonry, where, by a still more extraordinary coincidence, we also find among several strange and hard to interpret terms, the word *Salix*, meaning 'willow' in Latin; but just the same, we do not wish to draw any conclusions from this latter fact, which we mention simply as a curiosity. — As to the rice in the dipper, this evokes the 'vessels of abundance' common to various traditions, the best known example of which in the West is the *Grail*, and which also have a central significance (see *The King of the World*, chap. 5); rice here represents the 'food of immortality', which is also equivalent to the 'drink of immortality'.

11. This is no mere 'play on words', contrary to what Favre says; the dipper is really the very symbol of the Great Bear, just as the balance was in an earlier age, for according to the Far-Eastern tradition the Great Bear was called the 'Scales of Jade', that is to say, according to the symbolism of jade, Perfect Balance (moreover, the Great Bear and the Little Bear were assimilated to the two scales of a balance), before the name Balance was transferred to the constellation that now bears its name [Libra] (see *The King of the World*, chap. 10). [In English *Ursa Major* is commonly called the Big Dipper. The French word *boisseau*, here translated as 'dipper', means literally 'bushel' or 'corn-measure'. Ed.]

symbolically regarded as the dwelling-place of the seven *Rishis*, which makes it an equivalent of the 'Abode of the Immortals'. Moreover, since the seven *Rishis* represent the 'supra-human' wisdom of cycles anterior to our own, it is also a kind of 'ark' where is stored the deposit of traditional knowledge in order to assure its preservation and transmission from age to age.[12] In this, too, it is the image of the spiritual centers that have this function and, above all, of the supreme center which preserves the deposit of the primordial tradition.

On this subject we will mention another no less interesting 'polar' symbolism found in certain ancient rituals of Operative Masonry. In some of these rituals the letter 'G' is depicted at the center of the vault, at the very point corresponding to the Polestar;[13] a plumb-line suspended from this letter 'G' falls directly to the center of a *swastika* drawn on the floor, which thus represents the terrestrial pole.[14] This is the 'plumb-line' of the 'Great Architect of the Universe', which, suspended from the geometrical point of the 'Great

12. Rice (which is equivalent to wheat in other traditions) also has a meaning related to this same point of view, for food symbolizes knowledge, the first being assimilated corporeally just as the second is assimilated intellectually (see *Man and His Becoming according to the Vedānta*, chap. 9). Moreover, this meaning is directly connected to that we just noted, for it is traditional knowledge (understood in the sense of actual and not merely theoretical knowledge) that is the veritable 'food of immortality', or, according to the Gospel expression, the 'bread from Heaven' (John 6), for 'Man shall not live by [terrestrial] bread alone, but by every word that proceedeth out of the mouth of God' (Matt. 4:4; Luke 4:4), that is, in a general way, that comes from a 'supra-human' source. — Let us note in this connection that the expression *ton arton ton epiousion* in the Greek text of the Lord's Prayer does not at all signify 'daily bread', as it is usually translated, but quite literally 'supra-essential bread' (and not 'supra-substantial bread', as some say because of the confusion over the meaning of the term *ousia* that we noted in the first chapter of *The Reign of Quantity and the Signs of the Times*), or 'supra-celestial', if one takes Heaven as understood in its Far-Eastern sense, that is, as proceeding from the Principle itself and consequently providing man with the means of communicating with it.

13. On the other hand, the Great Bear is still depicted on the ceiling of many Masonic Lodges, even of the 'speculative' branch.

14. We would particularly call this to the attention of those who claim that we 'are making of the *swastika* the sign of the pole,' whereas we are only saying that this is in reality its traditional meaning; all the same, perhaps they will not go so far as to suppose that it was we ourselves who 'devised' the rituals of Operative Masonry!

Unity',[15] descends from the celestial pole to the terrestrial pole and is thus the figure of the 'World Axis'.

Having referred to the letter 'G', let us add that in reality this letter should have been the Hebrew *yod*, for which it was substituted in England as a result of phonetic assimilation of *yod* with 'God', which in any event does not fundamentally alter its meaning;[16] the various interpretations usually given to this letter (the most important being that which relates it to 'Geometry'), being for the most part only possible in modern Western languages, represent, whatever certain people may claim,[17] only secondary meanings that have incidentally gathered around this essential meaning.[18] The letter *yod*, the first letter of the Tetragrammaton, represents the Principle, so that it is regarded as constituting a divine name in its own right; by its form, moreover, it is the principial element from which are

15. In the Hebrew Kabbalah this is also the point from which the balance mentioned in the *Siphra Di Tzeniutha* is suspended [see *Traditional Forms and Cosmic Cycles*, pt. 2, chap. 5], for it is on the pole that the equilibrium of the world rests; and this point is designated as 'a place which is not', that is, as the 'non-manifest', corresponding, in the Far-Eastern tradition, to the assimilation of the Polestar as 'pinnacle of Heaven' to the 'place' of the Principle itself. This is also connected to what we said above about the scales in connection with the Great Bear. The two pans of the balance, with their alternating upward and downward movements, naturally refer to the vicissitudes of *yin* and *yang*; the correspondence of one side with *yin* and the other with *yang* is in a general way valid, moreover, for all double symbols having an axial symmetry.

16. The substitution of the 'G' for the *yod* is mentioned particularly, although not explained, in the *Récapitulation de toute la Maçonnerie ou description et explication de l'Hiéroglyphe universel du Maître des Maîtres*, an anonymous work ascribed to Delaulnaye.

17. There are even those who seem to believe that it was only after the fact that the 'G' was regarded as the initial letter in *God*. These people are obviously unaware of the fact of its substitution for *yod*, which is what gives it all its real significance from the esoteric and initiatic point of view.

18. In order to arrive at five different interpretations of the letter 'G', the recently instituted rites of the grade of Companion often give it meanings that are rather forced and insignificant; moreover, this grade has received more than its share of abuse, so to speak, as a result of the efforts made to 'modernize' it. — In its position at the center of the Blazing Star, the letter 'G' represents the divine principle residing in the 'heart' of the 'twice born' man (cf. *Perspectives on Initiation*, chap. 48).

derived all the other letters of the Hebrew alphabet.[19] It should be added that, as much by its rectilinear form as by its value as a Roman numeral, the corresponding letter 'I' of the Latin alphabet is also a symbol of Unity;[20] and it is curious to say the least that the sound of this letter is the same as that of the Chinese word *i*, which, as we have seen, also signifies unity, whether in its arithmetical sense or in its metaphysical transposition.[21] What is perhaps even more curious is that in his *Divine Comedy* Dante has Adam say that the first name of God, before it became *El*, was 'I'[22] (which implies, as we just explained, the 'primordiality' of 'polar' symbolism), and that in his *Tractatus Amoris*, Francesco da Barberino had himself portrayed in an attitude of adoration in front of the letter 'I'.[23] What this all signifies should now be easily understood: whether it is the Hebrew *yod* or the Chinese *i*, this 'first name of God', which in all probability was also the secret name of God among the *Fedeli d' Amore*, is in the final analysis nothing else than the very expression of principial Unity.[24]

19. As is well known, the numerical value of this letter is 10, and on this subject we refer the reader to what was said above [chapter 23] on the symbolism of the point at the center of a circle.

20. Perhaps we shall have occasion one day to study the geometrical symbolism of certain letters of the Latin alphabet and their use in Western initiations. [As far as we can determine, Guénon never devoted a separate study to this subject. ED.]

21. The character *i* is also a rectilinear stroke; it differs from the Latin letter 'I' only in that it is drawn horizontally rather than vertically. — In the Arabic alphabet, it is *alif*, the first letter of all and that numerically equivalent to unity, which has the form of a rectilinear stroke.

22. *Paradiso* XXVI: 133–4. — In an epigram ascribed to Dante, the letter 'I' is referred to as the 'ninth figure' in accordance with its position in the Latin alphabet, although the *yod*, to which it corresponds, is the tenth letter of the Hebrew alphabet; on the other hand, we know that the number 9 had a very particular symbolic importance for Dante, as is seen especially in his *Vita Nuova* (cf. *The Esoterism of Dante*, chaps. 2 and 6).

23. See Luigi Valli, *Il Linguaggio segreto di Dante e dei Fedeli d'Amore*, vol. 2, pp 120–121, where this picture is reproduced.

24. These remarks could have been used by those who have tried to establish a connection between the *T'ien Ti Huei* and Western initiations; but it is probable that they did not know of them, for they no doubt had hardly any exact information about Operative Masonry, and even less about the *Fedeli d'Amore*.

26

THE MIDDLE WAY

WE CONCLUDE this study with a final remark on the 'Middle Way'. We pointed out that this latter, identified with the 'Way of Heaven', is represented by the vertical axis considered in an ascending direction; but it is appropriate to add that this corresponds properly to the point of view of a being that, placed at the center of the human state, strives to raise itself from there to the higher states without yet having achieved total realization. On the contrary, when this being has identified itself with the axis by its 'ascension' along it up to the 'pinnacle of Heaven', it has so to speak thereby effectively led the center of the human state, which was its starting-point, to coincide for this being with the center of the total being. In other words, for such a being the terrestrial pole and the celestial pole are now one; and indeed this must be so since it has finally arrived at the principial state which is prior (if one can still use in this case a word evoking temporal symbolism) to the separation of Heaven and Earth. Thenceforward there is no longer any axis properly speaking, as if this being, in the measure that it is identified with the axis, had as it were 're-absorbed' it until it was reduced to a single point; but of course this point is the center which contains in itself all possibilities, not only of one particular state but of the totality of states manifested and unmanifested. It is only for other beings that the axis subsists such as it was, for there is no change in their state, and they remain in the domain of human possibilities; it is only with respect to them, therefore, that one can speak of a 're-descent' as we have done, and consequently it is easy to understand that this apparent 're-descent' (which is nevertheless also a reality in its own order) could not in any way affect 'transcendent man' himself.

The center of the total being is the 'Holy Palace' spoken of in the Hebrew Kabbalah, with which we have dealt elsewhere;[1] it is, one could say, continuing to use spatial symbolism, the 'seventh direction', which is not itself any specific direction but contains them all principially. It is also, to use another symbolism that we will perhaps have the occasion to explain one day, the 'seventh ray' of the Sun, that which passes through its very center, and, really being one with this center, can only be represented as a single point. It is again the true 'Middle Way' in its absolute sense, for it is this center alone that is the 'Middle Way' in all senses; and when we say 'sense' we do not mean only all the different meanings of which a word is susceptible, but also allude once again to the symbolism of the directions of space.[2] The centers of the different states of existence really only have the character of 'Middle' by participation and as it were by reflection, and consequently they have it only incompletely. If we turn again to the geometrical representation of the three axes of coordinates to which space is related, we can say that such a point is the 'Middle' with respect to two of these axes, which are the horizontal axes determining the plane of which it is the center, but not with respect to the third, that is, the vertical axis through which it receives this participation in the total center.

In the 'Middle Way' as we have just understood it, there is 'neither right nor left, front nor back, above nor below'; and we can readily see that for a being that has not yet reached the universal center, only the first two of these three pairs of complementary terms can cease to exist for it. Indeed, once a being has arrived at the center of its own state of manifestation, it is beyond all the contingent oppositions that derive from the vicissitudes of *yin* and *yang*,[3] so that

---

1. *The King of the World*, chap. 7; *The Symbolism of the Cross*, chap. 4.

2. The French *sens* signifies both 'meaning' and 'way' or 'direction'. ED.

3. Cf. *The Symbolism of the Cross*, chap. 7. — One could, if so inclined, take as the type of these oppositions that between 'good' and 'evil', but on condition that they be understood in their widest sense and not be restricted to the exclusively 'moral' meaning which they are normally given; still, this would be nothing more than one particular case, for in reality there are many other kinds of opposition which do not reduce to this one, for example those of the elements (fire–water, air–earth) and the sensible qualities (dry–wet, hot–cold).

henceforth there is no longer any 'right or left'; moreover, temporal succession has disappeared, transmuted into simultaneity at the central and 'primordial' point of the human state[4] (and the same will naturally apply to every other mode of succession, if it is a question of the conditions in another state of existence), and thus one can say, according to what we explained apropos of 'triple time', that there is no longer any 'front or back'; but there will always be 'above and below' with respect to that point, even with respect to the entire length of the vertical axis; and that is why this axis is the 'Middle Way' only in a relative sense. For there to be no 'above or below', the point at which the being is located must be effectively identified with the center of all states; from this point extends indefinitely in every direction the 'universal spherical vortex' of which we have spoken elsewhere,[5] which is the 'Way' along which the modifications of all things unfolds; but this vortex itself, being in reality only the unfolding of the possibilities of the central point, must be conceived as entirely contained in it principially,[6] for from the principial point of view (which is not a specific or 'distinctive' point of view), it is the center which is everything. That is why, according to Lao Tzu, 'the way which is a way [which can be traversed] is not the [absolute] Way,'[7] because, for the being that has actually established itself at the total and universal center, it is this unique point, and it alone, which is truly the 'Way' outside of which there is nothing.

4. Cf. *The Reign of Quantity and the Signs of the Times*, chap. 23.

5. *The Symbolism of the Cross*, chap. 20.

6. This is another instance of the symbolic 'reversal' resulting from the passage from the 'outward' to the 'inward', for this central point is obviously 'inward' with respect to all things, although, for the one who has reached it, there is no longer really any question of 'outward' or 'inward', but only an absolute and indivisible 'totality'.

7. *Tao Te Ching*, chap. 1.

INDEX